MID-TWENTIETH CENTURY NATIONALISM

J

WITHDRAWN

LEO M. FRANKLIN
1870–1948

MID-TWENTIETH
CENTURY
NATIONALISM

The Franklin Memorial Lectures

Volume XIII

Edited by WILLIAM J. BOSSENBROOK
Holder of the Leo M. Franklin Memorial Lectureship
in Human Relations at
Wayne State University for the year 1962–63

DETROIT—WAYNE STATE UNIVERSITY PRESS—1965

Published simultaneously in Canada by
Ambassador Books, Limited, Toronto, Ontario, Canada

Library of Congress Catalog Card Number: 65–11610

The lectures in this volume were broadcast locally by WDET (Wayne State University), nationally through the facilities of the National Association of Educational Broadcasters, and internationally by the Voice of America.

The Leo M. Franklin Lectures and the Holders of the
Leo M. Franklin Memorial Lectureship in Human Relations
at Wayne State University

† Out of print.   * To be published in 1966.

Titles of volumes differ in some instances from titles of lectures as originally announced.

Contents

Preface

The Leo M. Franklin Memorial Lectureship in Human Relations was established at Wayne State University in 1950 through the generosity and far-sighted civic patriotism of Temple Beth El, Detroit, Michigan. The members of Temple Beth El sought in this fashion to honor the memory of Dr. Leo M. Franklin, who served as rabbi from 1899 to 1941 and rabbi emeritus until his death in 1948, and who won national fame as well as the love and respect of his fellow-citizens of all faiths in Detroit through his championship of social progress and human decency for all Americans and all men everywhere.

Each year the Franklin Memorial professor, a member of the faculty recommended by a faculty committee and appointed by the president of Wayne State University, organizes and presents a series of lectures featuring significant contemporary aspects of human association.

This book presents the thirteenth annual series of the Franklin Lectures. The lectures are printed here essentially as they were given. Some slight modifications have been made to adjust the style of presentation to the reader.

I wish to take this opportunity to thank Temple Beth El, President Clarence Hilberry, and my colleagues for the honor conferred on me. I am also greatly indebted to my fellow lecturers for their collaboration in attempting to throw some light on an obscure but significant phenomenon of the modern political world.

WILLIAM J. BOSSENBROOK

Introduction

Introduction

It would appear from the titles of this lecture series that nationalism has not changed its spots since the nineteenth century. We are apparently still concerned with its traditional problems: with the unification of an ethnic group, as with the Germans; with the leadership role of a particular people, as with the French; with the treatment of minorities, as in the Soviet Union; with racial antagonisms, as in South Africa; and with self-determination among emerging nations, as in Mid-Africa.

Actually, the fundamental conditions under which twentieth-century nationalism is developing will bring about great changes in its essential character. *First,* and most obvious, the frame is no longer European but global —hence peoples not of just one culture but of many different religions and civilizations are now involved. *Second,* its power basis has changed with the development of new weapons of enormous destructive force, which are controlled at the moment by two colossal powers who virtually dominate the globe, thus giving new meaning to the concept of national sovereignty. *Third,* all over the globe man is becoming increasingly mobile—he is being cut loose from his old local, occupational, and class moorings which formerly gave stability to national and cultural communities.

It is apparent that all three factors—global frame, power basis, and geographical and social mobility—reflect the pervasive influence of technology, which is bringing about a fundamental revolution in man's sense of identity with the traditional time and space patterns embodied in communal forms.

Technology makes change seem not a historical development, in which old and new are in a continuous process of mutual adjustment, but a complete rupture with all past forms which are regarded as obsolete. Our sense of continuity with the past is wiped out most effectively through a total transformation of our immediate environment, where formerly continuity was most manifest. The demolition of old houses and public buildings, the widespread transformation of the landscape by great expressways, and the development of contemporary architecture which aims at total change, involving not only buildings but landscape and town planning—all bring about the loss of any actual contact with the past. We see the rubble of demolition but not the ruins of time, except when preserved as museum pieces and thus relegated to a contrived past which has no actual continuity with the present. Shortly, most of us will no longer be living in the houses, buildings, villages, and cities which in the past directly linked us with our forefathers.

Technological man, unlike traditional man, cannot accept the present as a mold or frame, more or less fixed, within which man has lived and will live indefinitely. Technological man never accepts any tool, habitation, or institution for its individual adequacy, but must always project a better model on the drawing board.

The old attachments to swimming holes, lovers' lanes,

6

haunted houses, old city halls and courthouses, which provided the local color of traditional patriotism, are displaced by the anonymity of recreational areas, forest preserves, national parks, and museums which are the scenes of organized activity. Hence classical patriotism, which looked inward to the defense of home and hearth, rocks and rills and templed hills, atrophies, and is displaced by a nationalism which looks outward to the assertion of the sovereign right of self-determination against all restrictions from without.

Nature retains no majesty or sovereignty by virtue of being inaccessible or unapproachable. There are no mountains that have not been climbed, or seas that have not been crossed in almost every conceivable variety of vehicle, or lands which the feet of the tourist have not trod. An atomic explosion far transcends nature's most violent moods as man encounters them. Man thus has no competitor in nature, no real physical and psychological limits to his self-assertion, either as an individual or a group. The Greek conception of cosmos and the accompanying notions of hubris and fate have disappeared. Technological man has only his own works and his fellow man as real limitations to his self-assertion.

A more positive picture of the relationship between technology and nationalism appears in what Adlai Stevenson called the "revolution of expectations." It recognizes no limitations to the advance of peoples by virtue of the traditional designations—barbarians, savages, or primitives—only that they are late-comers on the technological scene. Even the so-called advanced peoples have no substantive assurance of having "arrived," as is evident in their preoccupation with the rate of growth in terms of statistics of productivity, employment, and population increase. It has been aptly said that progress is no longer an aspiration but a fact, because we can measure it.

The emphasis laid on the total organization of labor, the immediate adoption of the most advanced technics, and the establishment of uniformity of wants, both in the advanced and in the developing technological societies, all contribute to the mobility increasingly characteristic of the twentieth-century world. One must be ready to move to a new locality or a different region in spite of the loss of friends or neighbors, to change one's occupation in spite of aptitude or interest, and to develop an "opportunism of taste" in spite of the fact that it may mean giving up the comforts of yesterday. All are necessary to keep up with one's time, to be contemporary. A discerning French writer puts it this way:

> This imperative calls for a reversal of all social values. That a man should have roots in one part of the world; that he should be attached to it because this is where the tombs of his ancestors are, the memories of his childhood and youth, the ties of blood and friendship, and in short, his loves and his duties; this has always been judged to be good, at all times and by all men. But it has now become an evil because it conflicts with the demands of productivity. The man who was firmly rooted in his soil and tied by blood and friendship to his neighbors was always the paradigm of a good citizen. He has now become a recalcitrant producer.[1]

What is required of the individual in this productive society is that he become "a docile nomad." Conformity to change takes the place of the age-old conformity to the status quo.

The peasantry have throughout history provided the

8

most stable basis of traditional culture. They furnished
the immovable base of the sacred empires of Egypt and
China which maintained remarkable stability and uniformity of institutions and customs over several thousand
years. To a given generation, changes appeared only with
the death or removal of the ruling personality or clique
and were thus, at most, palace revolutions. The peasant
in his village—following the endless cycle of tilling the
land and harvesting his crops, supported by mythical and
magical tradition going back in many cases to the neolithic
age—really had no history.

Only recently has this static mass been put into motion
and entrained in the revolutionary movement of history.
It may be that the most far-reaching social transformation
of the twentieth century was the uprooting of the peasant
masses in what were formerly the greatest agrarian countries of the world, namely Russia and China. Communism
in these countries aims primarily at organizing the total
population into a mobile labor force and thus overcoming
the inertia of a vast body of artisans and peasants.

Among all peoples the feeling of nostalgia for traditional values and stability is likely to grow in the face of
the increasing mobility and fluidity of the technological
order. The products of that order, even though available
in increasing numbers, give no lasting sense of adequacy in
terms of the amenities of human society—they merely
drive men on to demand an increasing number and variety
of objects to compensate for their basic qualitative in-
adequacy.

The claims of technology will of course be greatly reinforced by the demands of national sovereignty. On the
one hand global society is becoming technologically more

9

closely knit and complex and, on the other hand, the number of sovereign national entities, each presumably bent upon asserting its right to control its own affairs and to realize its individual interests and destiny, is also multiplying.

National self-determination is assuming both an old and a new guise under these conditions; old, in the sense that both the old and new nations are asking the pertinent question: Who but ourselves can be actually responsible for our own safety? New, in the sense that the feeling of safety no longer depends on the possession of adequate means of defense but is inherent in the potential danger of the weapons themselves to all possible belligerents.

On the one hand, the development of atomic power has become the symbol of technological advancement and the basic aspiration of national self-determination. On the other hand, the widespread dispersal of thermonuclear weapons is regarded as the greatest menace to the safety of mankind. This ambivalent situation has contributed enormously to the confusion of foreign policy, especially of the dominant powers.

In the Europe of the nineteenth and early twentieth centuries there existed but one fundamental distinction—there were the great powers and there were the small nations. The latter were practically ruled out of the area of decision making. In that system, substantive considerations such as territorial extent, population, economic resources, and geographical position made possible fairly accurate judgments of the relative power of the different states. But now the determining factors are really technological and psychological, and highly incalculable.

The initial development of nuclear power required

tremendous resources, but this limitation is likely to be largely overcome in the future. It now seems that the advances of technology in the realm of weapon systems will be appropriated by peoples of varying technological advance and material resources with increasing facility.

The psychological factor is equally disturbing. The essence of Italian fascism lay in the assumption that a fusion of wills under the driving force of a great leader would compensate for the lack of material resources, thus overcoming the "inferior" position of Italy. Likewise, in German National Socialism the fusion of minds and wills coming to focus in the charismatic leader joined with technological organization, would, it was assumed, enable the Germans to overcome the narrow limitations of their central European position. Again in communism, the party becomes the organized will for overcoming the industrial backwardness of a particular national group and for achieving a breakthrough to a "new order" of things.

The fluid character of the technological basis of national welfare and power therefore increasingly places a premium on the unity and uniformity of national self-assertion, and hence encourages totalitarianism in both the advanced and the underdeveloped countries.

With the breakup of the bipolar power structure, the waning of anti-colonialism, and the decline of ideologies, it would seem that we stand on the brink of a second wave of nationalistic self-assertion on a global scale. Will this wave gradually subside, as did the first European wave in the second half of the nineteenth century? Will it also lead to a new coalescence and alignment of forces culminating in great conflicts? Or will the movement toward common

11

markets, regional confederations, and total technological exploitation of the globe assume the upper hand? The following lectures may be called exercises in historical divination, directed toward revealing the ambiguities of the present world situation.

I

German Nationalism and Fragmentation

by

WILLIAM J. BOSSENBROOK

German Nationalism and Fragmentation

What some historians now call the second Thirty Years' War (1914–45) was the curtain-raiser on a process of national aggrandizement, social revolution, and technological change which is transforming the globe. The war began as a European hegemonial drive by the Germans; at its conclusion it had developed into a conflict for global preeminence between the peripheral peoples, the Americans and the Russians. The war produced a revolutionary movement which sought to establish a classless society directed by reason and justice rather than by power interests, but actually brought about rule by the "technicians of power" and the virtual liquidation of social justice ideologies. This conflict was a crusade to abolish war as a menace to civilization but produced a thermonuclear weapon which threatens the very existence of mankind.

This incongruity is generally attributed to the fact that in the course of the war social revolution and scientific technology took precedence over political and military considerations and directed it into channels far removed from the limited character of a mere European balance-of-power conflict. The war became global in scope and aimed at effecting a social revolution by turning not only the oppressed social groups against their exploiters but exploited peoples against their imperialist masters. Furthermore, it introduced into the conflict as weapons all the resources of science and technology formerly devoted to peaceful purposes. For these reasons the conflict of 1914–45 inaugurated what is really a global civil war. The first Thirty Years' War ended with a definitive peace treaty, the Peace of Westphalia (1648), in which the major powers laid down the ground rules of international order, so to speak, by virtually ruling out ideological differences as a factor in the conflict between states. Now, though the ideological factor may be declining in importance, the very variety and complexity of the technological means of conflict make peace indistinguishable from war.

Many discern in the "protracted conflict" the birth pangs of a global civilization reflecting the all-enveloping technical milieu. Some contend it has found its appropriate "political" order in the ideological conflict of the bipolar world of the USA and the USSR and their respective allies and satellites. Others argue that with the loosening of the two systems it is moving toward a multi-centered power-politics world like old Europe. Still others profess to see mankind eventually compelled to create a system of planned global exploitation by the exigencies of the population growth, of outer-space exploration, and of the menace of the bomb.

Obviously, the German question must be considered in the light of these perspectives of global order which are not mutually exclusive—in fact, they reflect different levels of international intercourse which exist contemporaneously.

In the seventeenth century, after the great devastation of the first Thirty Years' War (1618–48), it took more than a half century for the Germans to recover, economically and culturally. In the twentieth century their economic recovery—at least that of the West Germans—has been rapid and phenomenal, but some argue that it has been achieved at the cost of spiritual and cultural values. They again find themselves divided into two ideological camps but with this fundamental difference, that the ideological alignment follows a much more definite power-politics alignment than that between Protestants and Catholics in the seventeenth century.

One naturally asks these questions: Are the Germans again to remain an ideologically divided house, fragment-ized politically? Will the waning of ideological friction leading to the ascendancy of power-politics congeal the existing *de facto* partition of the Germans into viable po-litical units? Or will a nationalistic surge like National Socialism break out again, enveloping the Germans and turning them into a torrent bursting the dikes set up to contain it?

An attempt will be made to answer these questions, both by assessing the factors which made German nation-alism a revolutionary force in the twentieth century and by considering their present potential. Fundamental to the problem of unity was the Germans' view of their power position in central Europe, their conception of ethnic unity, and their adherence to a traditionalistic social order.

German historians of the late nineteenth and early twentieth centuries stressed the primacy of foreign affairs and power politics over domestic concerns and govern-mental structure as the determining forces of national destiny. They were under the spell of Bismarck's success-ful diplomatic and military strategy, which had made

17

German unification possible, with Prussia as its core. Hence the development of Brandenburg-Prussia, from the Great Elector in the seventeenth century to Bismarck in the nineteenth, was regarded as the model of what was required of a German nation-state in the way of maintaining itself and expanding its power in central Europe.

National unification around Prussia also made possible the evolutionary continuity of internal political and social structure centering in monarchical authority and traditional social hierarchy, which was thus maintained down into the twentieth century. Many German historians argued that the exposed position of the Germans in the middle of Europe made necessary a powerful military-bureaucratic state, with a stable authoritarian government and social structure, to serve as a fortress within whose walls German *Kultur* could preserve its distinctive character.

Two other conclusions were drawn from this power-politics orientation. It was argued that although religious and ideological conflicts on occasion assumed ascendancy over power interests and cut across state frontiers, the dynamics of the European state-system soon reasserted its determining influence. It was also assumed that this state system, based on the maintenance of a balance of power, would eventually be transferred to the globe, superseding English oceanic hegemony.

More zealous nationalists were convinced that this English hegemony was in process of decay and that the real decision as to world hegemony would be resolved by the Germans breaking out of the narrow confines of their continental position onto the open seas. The contrast between the consciousness of the great progress made by

Germans, particularly in science and technology, and of their cramped situation in central Europe in an age of imperialist expansion was the driving force behind this interpretation. It seemed that their situation was the penalty they suffered merely for arriving late on the scene as a national power.

The view that the European state system will be translated to the globe at large has been criticized by recent German historians—most cogently by Ludwig Dehio.[1] He contends that the balance-of-power dynamics operated "successfully" in the European cultural matrix because of common spiritual values and political mores, which provided the ground rules, and because the power struggles were confined to the European arena by British sea power, thus maintaining an equilibrium of power among four or five states. The great technological development of the peripheral peoples, the Americans and Russians, with their enormous resources, brought to an end the European-centered globe and created the bipolar global power-structure.

Dehio places the German hegemonial drive in new perspective by comparing it with previous thrusts, such as those of the Spanish in the sixteenth and seventeenth centuries and of the French in the seventeenth and eighteenth centuries. In the past, too much emphasis was placed on the maintenance of a balance or equilibrium among the four or five major powers within the European state system as an external rational order of thrust and counter-thrust and not enough on the inner irrational dynamics of the hegemonial drives themselves.

Each drive obviously assumed a character peculiar to the conditions of the age in which it occurred, but all together they reveal a cumulative character in which the demonry of power seeks, so to speak, complete realization. Hence each drive for domination manifests an increasing tendency toward a rising crescendo of violence, both external and internal, culminating in a climactic fusion of war and revolution.

The German thrust marked both the culmination and end of the successive hegemonial drives within the European system. It coincided with the emergence of a global field of forces in which mass ideologies and technological milieu are pulverizing and homogenizing traditional communal relationships and modes of behavior. The culminating phase, National Socialism, represented both an attempt of the Germans to break out of the continental European matrix and assume a global status and at the same time sought to make ethnic nationalism the all-inclusive cohesive force—the ersatz religion—of the new technological mass society.

In nazism the German hegemonial thrust therefore exhibited in an intensified degree the chief psychological traits of demonic power and of tragic hubris. First, nazism developed a tremendously inflated self-confidence, a sense of having arrived at a "supreme moment of destiny." Second, by repudiating the values of classical diplomacy and warfare reflecting concern for rational probabilities, enlightened self-interest, and civilized conduct, it succumbed to a "blind" use of power. Finally, it followed a deliberate policy of engendering hatred and hostility toward all "outsiders" without discrimination, thus seeking to promote a complete spiritual isolation of Germans from other peoples and indeed from the whole of the European Christian and cultural tradition. Nazists assumed that mankind was entering a new eon in which it was abandoning the historical world of European power politics and rational values and returning to the primordial world of racial conflicts for survival and mythical archetypes.

The basic conclusions drawn from this interpretation of hegemonial wars are that not only has the political power system which produced these hegemonial drives run its course, but the German hegemonial thrust has exhausted itself, as the Spanish and French did in the past. Are we then to assume that, in the new global situation of "protracted warfare," nationalism in its National Socialist totalitarian form of seeking an "ideal ethnic gestalt" has also run its course?

This ethnic ideal required, first, that substantially all Germans be brought together in one union, although they were scattered throughout middle Europe and intermingled, especially as one proceeded eastward, with many other peoples. Even the Austrians and Swiss, who spoke German and once were included in the Holy Roman Empire, should be included in a greater German union, even though they preferred their own individual national unions, established for many centuries. The fusion of the old Reich tradition with the concept of nationality is evident here.

Second, the ethnic ideal also implied that the union be one of minds and souls, thus constituting a *Volksgemeinschaft:* that is, a community based on an inner "spiritual" unity rather than on political mechanisms and procedures. Such a *corpus mysticum* obviously could not achieve adequate incarnation in a political structure. It did, however, as German historians stressed, become manifest in the sporadic national insurgency associated with such events

21

as the War of Liberation against Napoleon in 1813, the initial revolutionary wave of 1848, the united front at the outbreak of war in 1914, and perhaps again in the initial support given the Nazis in 1933–34. The earlier of these episodes, however evanescent in each of them the moment of true national cohesion, became great historic monuments in the works of German writers of history.

Finally, there was the traditional conception of the mission of the German people as the intermediaries between Western culture and the "barbarian" Slavs to the east. This concept of the preeminence of one people among others was not peculiar to the Germans and originally derived from a specific historical role played by a particular people. In the case of the Germans it harked back to the Holy Roman Empire, with its implication of the transfer of Roman sovereignty to the Germans and to their role as defenders of Western Christendom against barbarians and schismatics to the east.

But, in the democratic and imperialistic era of the late nineteenth and early twentieth centuries, the racial theory of indelible ethnic qualities was projected in response to the apparent need for ethnic common denominators in the emerging mass society and to the increasing contacts, via colonialism, with non-Western peoples and cultures. In place of the earlier conception of preeminence, based on ecumenical role, the concept of ethnic or racial superiority of one people over another now prevailed. Situated in the middle of Europe, many Germans were sensitive to both their ethnic vulnerability and superiority. To the west were the decadent Latins with their pretensions to cultural superiority and to the east the inferior Slavs who ruled over German minorities. The Germans were a young and vigorous people, coming late on the scene of world politics, but whose manifest destiny was to assume leadership in the twentieth century as they had in the great days of the Holy Roman Empire.

In terms of total comprehension, mystical communality, and cultural mission, German unity has been a potential ideal never adequately realized when compared with the medieval *sacrum imperium.* Its secular counterparts in recent times, such as the Second and Third Reichs, have been either a pale reflection or a demonic incarnation.

The dynamism of the *Volk* could never really find adequate realization in a given territorial or constitutional form. The second, or Bismarckian Reich, served as the chief historical model of German national unity for later regimes, including the present Federal Republic. It united the bulk of Germans and at the same time preserved the historic *Länder* such as Prussia, Bavaria, etc. It was also a cleverly contrived combination of liberal-democratic institutions, such as parliamentary representation, along with authoritarian monarchy and traditional social hierarchy. Actually, the Bismarckian Reich was a confederation of princes and free cities and not a national union in either the liberal-democratic or the romantic *Volksgemeinschaft* sense. In its republican counterpart, the Weimar Republic, the major functions of government were transferred from the monarchy to the parliamentary-party system. However, during the fifteen years of its existence, the hegemonial peoples of central and eastern Europe, the Germans and the Russians, were at the nadir of their power with respect to former subject peoples who established new nation-states.

Outwardly, the Third Reich came closest to realizing

the three facets of the ethnic ideal: inclusion of all Germans, a sense of inner community and restoration of hegemonial position. But the National Socialist movement, in combining the dynamism of the ethnic ideal with the hegemonial drive, increasingly subordinated the creative energies of the *Volk* to the demonry of power and directed them into mainly destructive channels. In the last phase of the regime, the dominance of the elite guard, the SS (*Schutzstaffel*), who were by no means all members of the Nazi party, is indicative of the complete ascendancy of the power motif over the ethnic ideal.

Although the Third Reich thus may have demonstrated the unrealizable character of the ethnic ideal of national unity, the latter remains a potential force to be reckoned with, particularly since it provides the ideal of a "single national identification" to uprooted and fragmented Germans in spite of differences of political allegiance and ideology. After all, not only are the Germans fragmentized, but one out of every five Germans in the Federal Republic is either a refugee or expellee from the eastern lands which Germans had occupied for centuries. But this consolidation of Germans, it also may be argued, may very well deprive the ethnic ideal of a chief motive force, namely that of bringing to an end the rule by alien inferiors over large numbers of Germans.

Both a counterforce to, and promotor of, hegemonic drive and ethnic dynamism was the traditional social hierarchy which persisted down to the Nazi regime. The variegated class pattern of the social hierarchy required the unifying image of the ethnic ideal to bind all Germans to the service of *Volk* and *Staat*.

In spite of what Prussian reformers from Frederick the

Great to Bismarck attempted in the way of defeudalizing and rationalizing the traditional monarchical military-bureaucratic structure, they deliberately did not alter the interwoven character of political structure and social hierarchy. They maintained the gentry's preeminence in military, diplomatic, and administrative affairs. While landholding became increasingly less important as an economic factor, it retained a great social prestige and local political authority for the East Elbean Junkers. Business, university, and church continued to be the peculiar spheres of the middle class. Even the industrial workers organized in trade union and socialist parties seemed to have achieved a modern counterpart to the medieval craft guilds.

A further buttressing of this social hierarchy was provided by the religious emphasis, inherited especially from the Reformation and later Pietist movements, on devotion to one's calling (*Beruf*) as one's divinely ordained position in society. The consequent German disposition to disciplined work is often cited as the major cause of German progress in science and technology. The gradual attenuation of the religious motivation behind profession and vocation was compensated for by the increased emphasis on devotion to state and nation. But with scientific and industrial expansion and the consequent increased emphasis on technical competence, the center of gravity naturally moved from the role of class to that of individual professional and vocational prestige, as it already had in the more fluid societies of the Western democracies.

Perhaps the most important positive contribution made by National Socialism was the dissolution of the traditional political-social hierarchy. It not only liquidated the gentry in a variety of purges, but it set up new hierarchies of party and economic organization alongside the traditional order; these merely served to emasculate the latter but provided no new sense of social order. In thus sapping the substance of both the social hierarchy and the religious imperative of calling, National Socialism greatly contributed to the mobility necessary to changing technological needs. Though not revolutionary in the traditional sense of directly supplanting one political and social order with another, National Socialism nevertheless recognized the "twentieth century revolution" as being technological; that is, functionally rational and not ideologically so. It recognized, at least implicitly, that the ideologies of the previous age were utopian in their assumption that the aspirations and ideas of a social group could anticipate future basic changes in society. Actually, the latter must wait upon technological developments whose political and social implications are ambiguous.

The German thus finds himself in a situation where he realizes that the traditional frames of *Staat, Volk* and *Beruf* no longer provide the guidelines of his existence. There are in fact no historic frames in which power politics, national aspiration, and professional career can find direction. One exists in what seems to be an indefinitely prolonged interim which requires no historical explanation, as would a new political and social order, but waits upon the day by day changes in the situation. There is no longer a past or future to be reconciled historically, merely an everlasting present. Total immersion in the present obviously makes for indifference toward explaining the inhumanities and barbarities of the Hitler regime. They actually seem as remote as the atrocities and cannibalism

26

attributed to the first Thirty Years' War. In any case, during the Nazi regime, one still lived in a world where one was strictly subject to orders from above and where duty to vocation, class, and nation were all-absorbing obligations. That world passed in a series of great cataclysmic changes; now one feels no responsibility for it, particularly as one recognizes today that people are largely the puppets of impersonal forces. The attempt on the part of certain academicians to build on the precedent of the resistance movement to Hitler an "inner spiritual resistance" to the magic of slogans and catchwords and to blandishments of national pretension and vainglory, and thus create a renewed sense of inner responsibility of an existential character, seems highly esoteric in our society of mass media of communication.

Much more expedient is the activity of the irrepressible power-politics historians, both German and non-German, who are seeking to exorcize the Nazi demons. They argue either that Hitler was actually forced into going to war, or that his objectives were not basically different from those of his German predecessors. Thus the continuity of history as past politics is maintained and is extended into the present by those who assert that the bipolar world, based on the conflict between the Communist world and the free world, is dissolving into the normal situation of a multi-centered world dominated by the clash of power interests. Presumably the traditional power interests of the Germans will manifest themselves again in a drive toward national unity which, in view of their position in central Europe, will also mean an attempt to restore their hegemonial position there.

There are also the proponents of the continued ascendancy of the world-wide ideological conflict who believe that this conflict has by no means really abated except on the surface, that it is being fought with sophisticated weapons no longer adapted to an overt ideological confrontation on a global scale but adjusted to the varying local conditions of the conflict. National movements, whether as revolts initiated against Western colonialism or, as in the case of the Germans, for national re-unification, reflect the impact of the global conflict. Since the Germans occupy a strategic position where the line of conflict cuts across them both geographically and ethnically, their situation is obviously crucial.

In any case, whether one follows the power-politics or ideological orientation, the German problem in its immediate aspect must be considered first of all from the point of view of the viability of the German Democratic Republic (East Germany) and especially of the Federal Republic of Germany (West Germany) which, in the eyes of most, is the more likely to serve as a nucleus of national unity. Some argue, however, that too much emphasis has been placed on the relatively greater industrial progress and prosperity of the West Germans, which may be ephemeral and is in fact showing signs of slowing down. It is difficult to determine the degree of antipathy or sympathy felt by the East Germans toward the ruling Communist regime. It will undoubtedly relax its repressive character in time, as those in Czechoslovakia and Poland already have, especially with the passing of Ulbricht. In any case, that regime has produced a ruling German elite in the approximately twenty years of its existence which has become adept in the use of instruments of power to maintain its position. It is moreover associated, at least indirectly, with the élan of a revolutionary movement while the Federal Republic is, if anything, counter-revolutionary. As far as national posture is concerned, both regimes suffer from the stigma of having been imposed from the outside, and neither seems more likely than the other to recover the lands east of the Oder-Neisse line.

While the Federal Republic has shown amazing economic and technical progress, many observers point out that it suffers from basic political weaknesses. It lacks a definite political tradition and complete constitutional character. At its establishment it was thought of as having an interim character, since it was then assumed that with the end of the occupation the Germanies would be reunited, which might require a fundamental modification of the political structure. It was merely equipped, therefore, with the necessary governmental apparatus.

To prevent seizure of power via democratic processes in the manner of the Nazis, a system of checks and balances was set up, in which a strong executive was contraposed to party domination through parliament and a federal organization of states was to serve as a counterpoise to a unitary state order. The architect of this political structure was Konrad Adenauer, who thought of it as a return to the basic operational principles of a modernized Bismarckian Reich, and whose foreign policy was European power-politics oriented, rather than geared to the global conflict between the USA and the USSR. Most important, during the long period of his chancellorship, Adenauer, like his predecessor, stamped his personality on it, thus bequeathing to his successors a dubious political heritage. The present Federal Republic lacks both the Prussian and monarchical tradition of the Bismarckian

Reich and at the same time is not connected even indirectly with a revolutionary tradition.

Nevertheless, the very provisional and artificial character of the Federal Republic provides it with qualities suitable to the technological milieu, where all power arrangements and politico-social forms are increasingly felt to have an interim character. Moreover, unlike the Weimar Republic, it does not suffer from the stigma of a lack of harmony between its structure and the national tradition or ethos, since it does not presume to be an embodiment of the latter. The very fact that it lacks a definite national and constitutional character provides an element of strength in a world where traditional national sovereignty and the nation as "one and indivisible" may be passing from the scene. It will likely establish closer relations with its East German counterpart, but a national consolidation is extremely unlikely, not merely because of the global power conflict which cuts across the German sector, but because each political structure has developed its own ruling elite. Each has vested power interests and varying traditions—the one communistic revolutionary, the other traditionalist counter-revolutionary. A nationalist movement, independent, so to speak, of both political structures also is unlikely to gain a foothold in the foreseeable future. This political fragmentation conforms to the general trend toward federative structures, such as the Soviet Union and the incipient European union, in which the large-scale ethnic political entities do not fit—except as a hegemonial axis, as in the Soviet Union.

The divergence between traditional conceptions and aspirations and political and technological realities is most apparent as it pertains to the problems of national unification. Some commentators still assume an inevitable movement toward German reunification as if it is an irresistible natural phenomenon. They are still under the influence of the nineteenth-century European unification movements, in a world which has undergone a fundamental transformation as to power relations and ethnic considerations. Others argue that since the particularism of states and *Länder* rather than national unity has played the most enduring role in modern German history, therefore the present division of Germans does not constitute, so to speak, a historic violation of the principle of national unity. There is, of course, a considerable difference between pre-Bismarckian territorial-state particularism, reflecting the contests for political autonomy and hegemony within the old Holy Roman Empire, and present day national fragmentation, which has come as the aftermath of the drive for ethnic integration culminating in National Socialism.

National fragmentation, as distinct from state particularism, is not a new phenomenon in German history. In early modern history it was apparent in the crumbling of the Germanic world at the edges. The Swiss and the Dutch were the first to assume cultural autonomy, then political independence. Most recently, the Austrian Germans have detached themselves from the main bulk of Germans and have acquired a definite feeling of nationality. Likewise an East German national consciousness will no doubt appear among the erstwhile Prussian Germans within the orbit of the Soviet sphere. The West Germans will doubtless continue to regard themselves as the true core of German nationality, if for no other reason than that they outnumber the East Germans more than three to one and occupy more than twice the area of the German Democratic Republic. However, the West Germans of the

31

Rhineland and South may be disposed, by virtue of a dominant Catholicism and consequent cultural associations, to develop a feeling of national separation of their own. The loosening of the ties of the East Germans—as of the Poles and Czechs—with the Soviet Union and the development of a freer exchange of population and goods with the West is likely to facilitate this process toward what may be called national cultural particularism, since these exchanges would implicitly recognize the enduring character of the separate political entities.

There is, of course, the ever-present possibility that one or the other of these former fragments of the old Reich will claim to embody the true German ethnic gestalt and will again seek to combine them under its aegis in a great German national union. In assessing this probability we are again confronted with the ambivalent character of the main force of our time, the enveloping technological milieu. On the one hand, it tends to polarize rational functional organization and irrational quests for charismatic leadership and archetypical images, as National Socialism has already demonstrated. On the other hand, the expanding technological order also creates a common environment in which regional cultural distinctions tend to be effaced and collaborative effort in various associations cutting across national frontiers is enhanced.

Hence in this new technological milieu it is not a question of either-or, of complete national union or fragmentation, but of degrees of association on various levels of political, economic, scientific and cultural conflict and collaboration. Thus the vertical axis of a technological *ordo* may displace the horizontal and historical drive toward national self-realization.

II

French Nationalism and Western Unity

by

HANS KOHN

French Nationalism and Western Unity

Modern nationalism and the struggle for modern political liberty on the continent of Europe drew their inspiration largely from the French revolutions of 1789, of 1830, and of 1848. But in France herself the rights of men and of citizens and the parliamentary democracy, for which the Revolution of 1789, under the influence of English and Anglo-American liberal ideas, was originally fought, have never been securely established. Soon after 1791 the liberties of a modern free nation were curtailed or abolished by the dictatorships of Robespierre and of Napoleon I, who both claimed to save the nation and to re-establish its political and cultural leadership in Europe. The great majority of the French accepted with enthusiasm Napoleon's military dictatorship and his expansive and expensive wars, because he enhanced French *gloire* and prestige to an unprecedented degree. When he returned from Elba in 1815 to re-establish the empire, most Frenchmen welcomed him. The fall of Napoleon was followed by the return of the Bourbons, but the young French generation continued to dream of the bellicose achievements of Napoleon, of the French battle flags being carried all over Europe, of Paris as the capital of the globe.

The French monarchy ended in 1848, and the Second Republic established democratic liberties and introduced universal suffrage. But only for a short time; the warlike character of French nationalism and the bitterness of social conflicts in France were so strong, that in free general elections Napoleon's nephew was elected president of the republic. His success was based on his name, on the fear of socialism among the propertied classes, and on the promise of *gloire* and grandeur; three years later he could abolish democracy and the republic and restore a military dictatorship. Like Napoleon I, Napoleon III was not overthrown by resistance at home, but by defeat at the hands of foreign armies. After many hesitations and attempts at reintroducing some form of monarchy, the Third Republic emerged and showed an unexpectedly long life. The provisional constitution of 1875 remained in force until 1940. But the republic was never fully accepted by all Frenchmen; it was several times endangered by domestic crises. The Third Republic was able to overcome these crises, however, and France retained her role as leader of the European continent for many decades, not only in the arts and letters but also as a bastion of parliamentary democracy and civil liberty.

It must not be forgotten, however, that French nationalism differed fundamentally from nationalism in Great Britain, in the United States, or in Switzerland. In these countries the modern political order of an open free society, recognizing diversity and looking toward the future, had been freely accepted by the overwhelming majority of the nation. Each nation was based upon a compact, recognized by all, embodied in its constitution. No attempt was made in Britain after 1688, in the United States after 1788, in Switzerland after 1848, to go back to *l'ancien regime*, to a past preceding these constitutions, to install a pre-modern authoritarian government, to allow the military caste and mind (which hardly existed in these truly free modern nations) a decisive influence on the political life of the nation.

Things were different in France even after the fall of Napoleon III. There, parliamentary democracy and the party system were often held up to derision. They and the constitution did not take deep root in French public consciousness. Salvation was often sought in a strong man on horseback, elevated by the army to solitary authoritarian power, a man who would symbolize, not the spirit of the shopkeeper nations—a spirit which allegedly threatened to undermine the virtue of the French nation—but France's dignity, her military glory, and her claim to European hegemony. These aspirations found their expression in the widespread popularity of General Boulanger and in the bitterness of the Dreyfus affair, which amounted almost to a civil war between civilian republican democracy and the forces of *l'ancien regime*—the army, the church, the aristocracy. It was then that in the *Action Française,* in Charles Maurras and Maurice Barrès, the first fascist ideas were propagated in Europe.

In the 1920's, after victory in World War I, French nationalism tried to re-establish its hegemony on the European continent, from the Atlantic Ocean to the Vistula and the Black Sea. It fought its colonial wars in Morocco and in Syria, and regarded the British everywhere as the chief competitors for leadership. There was mutual distrust among the Western nations and no Franco-British collaboration existed to insure the continuation of the peace and the extension of liberty after 1918. This disagreement was one of the factors which contributed to the

37

rise of fascism and the weakening of democracy on the
European continent and, above all, in France herself.
Fascist and Communist influences gained rapidly in
France and helped bring about the collapse in 1940 of the
famous French army in an unprecedented debacle. In the
midst of her total defeat, France in her provincialism
could not imagine then that Britain would hold out. The
importance of maritime power, the cohesiveness and
morale, the strength and resilience of a truly democratic
nation were as little understood by many Frenchmen as by
many Germans. The majority of Frenchmen turned in
1940 to an old soldier who represented glorious memories
of the last war, to Marshal Henri Pétain. In his rise to
power and in his regime the forces defeated in the Dreyfus
affair found their revenge. French democracy was abolished, the parliamentary parties were discredited, and an
authoritarian regime by a man on horseback established,
a man who tried to turn the French mind back to its past,
to the supposed virtues, greatness, and glory of a France
not yet undermined by British ideas of liberal democracy.

With the help of Great Britain and the United States,
the French Republic, now called the Fourth Republic, was
re-established in 1944. Many leading Frenchmen understood that the time for French hegemonial aspirations had
passed, that France should accept wholeheartedly its new
role in a new Europe and in a new world. But many
Frenchmen suffered from the loss of prestige in 1940, nor
would they accept the change in the world position of
Europe. The British bowed out of their global imperial
position—by far the greatest of modern times—with some
good grace and wisdom and started the colonial peoples
on their road to independence by the example which they

set for Asia in 1947 in India, and for Africa in 1957 in Ghana. The French fought bitter and often cruel colonial wars to maintain their empire—first in Indochina, then in Algeria. This imperialism undermined the otherwise promising Fourth Republic which had launched an economic modernization of France. A revolt of the French Army in Algeria in 1958 overthrew the Fourth Republic and elevated General Charles de Gaulle, a dedicated nationalist and a shining symbol of French military *gloire* and grandeur, to a towering command position in France. His plebiscitary-authoritarian regime, which combined elements of the ancient monarchy of the grand *siècle* and of the Napoleonic tradition, and adapted them adroitly to the needs of modern times, was politely called the Fifth Republic, hereby denuding the democratic republican tradition of its true meaning. All real power in France was now in the hands of one man, and one man alone, though highly civilized and personally of exceptional moral integrity. In an age of resurgent democracy, in a Europe newly freed from despotism, how could democracy receive such a decisive blow as it did in France, a country widely believed to be a stronghold of democracy on the European continent?

In 1945 a chapter of European history came to an end. The days of European hegemony in the world and of the aspirations of a single European power for hegemony on the European continent seemed gone forever. Thanks to American aid—and France received a greater share than either Britain or West Germany—Europe quickly recovered. A leading German historian, Ludwig Dehio, warned as long as ten years ago—it was in June, 1953—in the German periodical *Aussenpolitik* that "the recovery of

Western Europe, which we owed to America, led to the resurgence of all our old nationalisms," and might lead to an undermining of the Atlantic Community and to the resurgence of European hegemonial struggles. This danger was especially great, Dehio insisted, among the two continental powers with a long military tradition and with old hegemonial aspirations, France and Germany. Germany has apparently learned the lesson of 1945 better than France did. World War I dealt a traumatic shock to German nationalism; World War II and its aftermath—the loss of the empire which France could not take with wisdom and grace as the British did—dealt a similar shock to the French. They found General de Gaulle, a man of great stature, totally dedicated to the revival of an outdated French national grandeur. He had no use for the new ways of supranational order, the United Nations and the Atlantic Community.

The appearance of the Fifth Republic in 1958 marked a strong reassertion of authoritarian and self-centered nationalism. French sovereignty in its fullest meaning became one of the most frequently emphasized claims of the new regime. It stresses not the interdependence of the West but the traditional lonely grandeur of France as the leader of Europe. This grandeur, many Frenchmen maintain, has been undermined since the eighteenth century by the competition of a commercialized Britain. This anti-British feeling dominated the French revolutions of the 1790's, the era of Napoleon, and even French liberals like Victor Hugo and Jules Michelet in the 1840's. After 1815 the French sought revenge for Waterloo and a rapprochement with Germany which they assumed would be led by France as the core of Europe against the two less-European powers—England and Russia. Again, Anglo-French rivalry was an important factor in preventing the consolidation of peace after World War I. It dominated the mentality of the Vichy regime. The retreat of France from her colonial positions, in Syria and Lebanon, in Morocco and Tunisia, has been attributed by French nationalists to intrigues or pressures promoted by Britain and the United States— even to a desire by these powers to take over France's imperial position in Africa, in the Middle East, and in Indochina.

The extreme nationalism which triumphed in France and in French Algeria in 1958 is perhaps the most dangerous expression of similar trends of a self-centered and self-assertive nationalism found to a lesser degree almost everywhere today, a trend also well known to us in the United States. This trend runs counter not only to the development of a world order but also to a healthy growth of democracy. In France one of her leading political scientists, Raymond Aron, asked in the monthly *Preuves* as early as July, 1959, the question, *"La democratie a-t-elle un avenir en France?"* and his answer was more than cautious. France today is passing through a crisis similar to that of the last years of the Weimar Republic in Germany. As for the United States, Britain, or Scandinavia, we know, almost with certainty, that their regimes will be fundamentally the same in five or ten years as they are today. I believe the stability of the German Federal Republic is assured even after Dr. Adenauer's overdue resignation. In France, on the other hand, no one knows what will follow General de Gaulle's relinquishment, presumably either through resignation or death, of his position of exalted loneliness and authoritarian leadership.

41

In his famous declaration of January, 1963, President de Gaulle virtually excluded—in the name of "Europe" and of "European civilization," but without any consultation with his European allies and in a rather strange definition of Europe—Britain from partnership in the Common Market. He did this not for economic reasons, in which he is little interested, but for the sake of his dream of French hegemony, which has inspired all his plans and guided all his actions for over twenty years, and specifically for the sake of the undoing of the defeat and debacle of 1940. It came as something of a surprise to many. This shows how little they have tried to understand the historical source of this declaration—its roots are in French nationalism and especially in that influential part of French nationalism which played a role in the election of Louis Napoleon, in the Dreyfus affair, and in the overthrow of the Fourth Republic, a nationalism of which General de Gaulle is the most august, impressive, and personally impeccable embodiment. His declaration of January, 1963, was not merely a tactical maneuver in reaction to the strategy of his nominal allies—the declaration has been interpreted as a reaction against the decisions of the conference at Nassau in the preceding month —but the culmination of a consistent policy toward supranational organizations—whether it be a really federated Europe of liberal democracies, a North Atlantic Community, or the United Nations. This was a policy of very long standing which goes back to 1940 and explains why the General in the years of World War II was such a difficult ally for President Roosevelt and Prime Minister Churchill.

In his *Memoirs,* which are a beautifully written monument to his aspirations and establish his place in history, the General unfolded his plan for the rehabilitation of French power and prestige. In the third volume, *Le Salut* (*Salvation*), published in French in 1959 and in an English translation in 1960, he wrote thus about the situation in 1944, after the liberation of France by predominantly American and British armies:

> No sooner had the sound of gun fire faded than the world's appearance changed. The strength and spirit of the peoples mobilized for the war suddenly lost their unifying object, while the ambition of states reappeared in all its virulence. The Allies revoked those considerations and concessions they had necessarily granted each other in time of peril, when they were confronting a common enemy. Yesterday was the time for battle; the hour for settling accounts had come.
>
> This moment of truth revealed France's continuing weakness in relation to her own goals and to the partisan calculations of other states. The latter, of course, would take advantage of the situation to try to force our hand on those issues still undecided, or else to relegate us to a secondary place among nations responsible for constructing the peace. But I had no intention of letting this happen. Considering, in fact, that Germany's collapse, Europe's laceration, and Anglo-American friction offered a miraculously saved France exceptional opportunities for action, it seemed likely that the new period would permit me to achieve the great plan I had conceived for my country.

To the reader it seems that the General, an ardent nationalist, reads into American and British actions the same unconditional and dedicated pursuit of purely nationalist goals, the same self-centeredness which he himself

43

so fervently feels for France. He is really a *grand doctrinaire*. British and American statesmen were much more pragmatic than he or other continental *doctrinaires* assumed or could even imagine. Britain and the United States had no plan for taking ruthless advantage of French —or Italian or German—weakness. The United States helped to put France and other countries of liberated Europe on their feet and supported the idea of a united Europe, even pushed the European nations towards concluding as close and firm a union as possible, of course without wishing Germany or France or any other European nation to strive for hegemony and leadership in such a united Europe.

Most revealing is the General's phrase a "miraculously saved France." To the joy of all free men France, beloved France, was saved, not by a miracle like that accomplished by Joan of Arc, but by the courage, the perseverance, the greatness, and the humanity of the British people in what Churchill called their finest hour. For many months they stood alone facing the terrifying might of Hitler, before Hitler's own actions brought the Russians and the Americans to Britain's side. During this time, de Gaulle conceived the "great plan," which he has tried to realize with model patience and supreme tactical skill for the last twenty years:

> I intended to assure France security in Western Europe by preventing the rise of a new Reich that might again threaten its safety; to co-operate with East and West and, if need be, contract the necessary alliances on one side or the other without ever accepting any kind of dependency; . . . to persuade the states along the Rhine, the Alps, and the Pyrenees [Germany, the Low Countries, Italy, and

Spain] to form a political, economic, and strategic bloc; to establish this organization as one of the three world powers and, should it become necessary, as the arbiter between the Soviet and Anglo-American camps. Since 1940 my every word and act had been dedicated to establishing these possibilities.

In 1944 the General was determined that no one should ignore or defy the will of France, especially not her allies. The first test came on the Franco-Italian border where France demanded the annexation of some small border territories. A tense moment followed, and the source of it was, according to the General, "the United States' desire for hegemony, which they readily manifested and which I had not failed to discern on every occasion. But above all, I perceived in their demand the effect of British influence. For at the same moment, England was preparing her decisive maneuver in the Middle East."

"I had always expected it," the General continues in a manner which reveals much more of his own nature and policy than of British intentions, "for the national ambitions masked by the world conflict included the British plan to dominate the Middle East. How many times I had already confronted this passionate resolve that was prepared to shatter any barrier that stood in its way!" (Here again the General speaks introspectively rather than from any true discernment of British "passions.") According to the General, the British were maneuvering to control the trade and the policies of the Middle Eastern states. Even in 1958 he forgets to add that Britain today controls the Middle Eastern states as little as France does, and that this revival of bygone rivalries in former colonial territories can hardly further the grandeur of France, for which the General cares most, or the unity of the West, for which he cares less.

Many people speak today of an Atlantic relationship based upon two pillars—the one formed by a United Europe, which however does not yet exist and of which few real traces are to be found in the hearts of most Europeans, and the other formed by the United States of America. These people forget or overlook the existence of Canada, which is an essential factor on the North American continent and in the North Atlantic Community, and which has played and will continue to play an important diplomatic role, both in the Western world and on a global scale. North America actually falls as short of being united as Europe does. The distrust of the United States felt in Canada or Mexico is comparable to that felt in many European countries toward France or Germany, toward their actual or possible hegemonial aspirations. This distrust of the United States by Canada is not a new phenomenon. More than twenty years ago a North American historian, the late Professor J. Bartlett Brebner of Columbia University, defining the relationship between his country of birth (Canada) and his country of adoption (the United States), pointed out in 1941 that "no great power seems habitually to be tender, imaginative, or subtle toward a weaker one, even when it is a neighbor. It is true, on the other hand, that the weaker powers are endlessly sensitive, subtle, and imaginative toward their overpowering neighbors. . . . Canada had always had to fear the expansive energies of the United States, whether in the overt forms of national and filibustering invasions, or in the peacetime pressure of economic policy and dollar diplomacy."

46

Similar to this oversensitive Canadian fear of the United States is the European fear of a Franco-German hegemony and the distrust felt for the United States by many Europeans, a distrust today weakest in the small countries, and strongest in France under the wholehearted inspiration of President de Gaulle, and of the propaganda dispensed by the state-owned television and radio. The fear of American civilization corrupting the higher and purer culture of old Europe is not new. At the beginning of this century a British journalist, William Thomas Stead, a contemporary of Theodore Roosevelt and Woodrow Wilson, wrote a book with the significant title *The Americanization of the World or the Trend of the Twentieth Century.* He raised issues which half a century later have become obvious— he spoke of the Americanization of European literature and art, marriage and society, habits of life and ways of consumption. He even spoke of an "American invasion" which he said then was bitterly resented by many Europeans "as if the Americans bearing gifts in their hands were bent upon doing us the greatest possible injury." He found continental Europe even more frightened than England; most hostile to this Americanization were the Germans, who wished to rally the continent against the United States, under the slogan "Europe for the Europeans," with Africa and Asia constituting the European reserves. But Stead regarded such European solidarity against the United States as a vain dream.

Today all lovers of freedom and of modern Western values, in terms of an open forward-looking society, based upon diversity and tolerance, will care for the strengthening of the North Atlantic Community and not for the assertion of hegemony, or the promotion of a self-centered

47

nationalism bound to the past and arousing illusions about the present. It was the fear of Soviet aggression which in 1949 made the creation of NATO possible. But today this fear of Soviet military aggression in Europe is largely gone, not on account of Western European strength, as General de Gaulle seems to think, and not on account of Soviet pacifism, but due to the protective power of the United States. Today the Atlantic Community is not primarily, though this was its origin, a defensive military alliance; it should be a means for the growth of democratic liberty and welfare in the Western world and beyond.

A final word about the Franco-German treaty of January 22, 1963, signed by Dr. Konrad Adenauer and General Charles de Gaulle. It confirms only an existing trend, without adding to it. The Germans desire close co-operation and friendship with France, whether with or without treaty, but most of them reject any exclusive treaty with France, any *directoire* of Europe, exercised by these two powers, guiding free Europe away from close co-operation with Britain and the United States. The Germans wish no exclusive treaty with France, but a friendship with all North Atlantic countries, and they know that close contact with the present authoritarian nationalist regime in France, with its contempt for parliamentary government and for political parties, cannot strengthen democracy in Germany, and may even reawaken the latent German-centered nationalism and authoritarianism. Rather, Germany has to look for democratic inspiration to Britain, Scandinavia, and the Low Countries—countries where democracy has been firmly rooted for generations, where it has stood the test of time. A closer union with the English-speaking peoples might also strengthen democracy in France and provide it with greater stability than it has shown in the last decades.

France's hegemonial aspirations are based upon ancient traditions to which no present reality corresponds. But France is not the only country in the Western world where hegemonial aspirations predominate and where they present a hindrance on the road to European and Atlantic co-operation. In France hegemonial aspirations are historically deep-rooted; in the United States they are not; nevertheless, the great strength of this country has led it in recent years to act often in a hegemonial way. It tends sometimes to treat its partners without full consideration. The insistence by the Congress on exclusive control of nuclear forces hardly inspires confidence in the co-operative spirit of the United States. There is much too little consultation between the United States and its partners in political, military, and economic matters. What the Franco-German treaty foresees for the institutionalization of Franco-German co-operation should be incorporated not in bilateral exclusive treaties, but in multi-lateral treaties binding all the nations of the North Atlantic Community together in consultation and co-operation, in their hearts and habits, yet at the same time respecting the cultural and historical diversity which is one of the great strengths of the free world, which in principle is an open outward-looking society, based upon pluralism and the recognition of the equality of strong and weak alike.

III

The Problem of National Minorities in the USSR

by
ALFRED G. MEYER

The Problem of National Minorities in the USSR

A short lecture on the problem of national minorities in the USSR can do no more than summarize existing knowledge and already formulated opinions of other scholars who have dealt with it. My aim is not to add a definitive contribution to such knowledge and opinions, but to enlighten an audience and a reading public which otherwise might not have occasion to learn about the problem under discussion.

The Union of Soviet Socialist Republics is a multinational society. I am tempted to call it a melting pot of nations and by the use of this term imply similarities between multi-national Russia and multi-national America. I shall return to this image, but for the time being I prefer to abandon it because, even though Americans come, directly or indirectly, from many different cultures and nations, the dissimilarities between the two societies are too great to be obscured by the use of a word which we customarily apply to our own country. The most important differences, perhaps, are the following:

1) While linguistic differences linger on in American society, we can say, on the whole, that all Americans speak one and the same language. This is not the case in the USSR.

2) By and large, cultural, religious, and racial differ-

53

ences in the Soviet Union are greater than in the United States.

3) At the same time, none of the cleavages in Soviet societies is quite so deep as that between Negroes and whites in America; nor are racial prejudice or racial discrimination significant elements in the attitudes and behavior of the Soviet population.

4) Finally, the nationalities problem in the USSR is distinct from that in the USA because the most important national minorities are not distributed evenly throughout the country. Rather, they are concentrated in various areas on the western and southern frontiers of the Soviet Union, forming distinct national areas or regions, in which Russian nationals have in the past constituted, and may still today be constituting, the minority population.

As of 1959, slightly over three-fourths of the country's population, or about 160 million people, were of Slavic origin; and among these, 115 million were Great-Russians; 37 million Ukrainians, and eight million Bielorussians. Slightly less than one-eighth of the population, or about 25 million, were Muslims, living in central Asia, along the lower Volga, in the north Caucasus region, and scattered in many other places. Most but not all of these Islamic nationalities speak Turkic languages. Other sizable minorities are the Georgians and Armenians in the Transcaucasian provinces; Poles, Moldavians, Latvians, and Lithuanians in the west; Estonians, Finns, and Chuvash in the northwest; Mongols and Koreans in the far east; and Jews throughout the western portion of the Soviet Union. Small contingents of many different nationalities, from Eskimos to Gypsies, are scattered through various areas of the country.*

These various nationalities speak different languages and have widely divergent cultures. Some of the small tribes of Siberia and the Arctic until recently lived near the level of Stone Age civilization. On the other hand, Armenians and Georgians look back to a long and proud autonomous cultural tradition. The teeming cities of southern central Asia have preserved some of the cultural flavor of medieval Islam, while the grasslands further north, only a generation ago, were the home of equally traditional Muslim nomad tribes. Whereas these and other Soviet nationalities clearly belong to Asia, the Poles and the Baltic nationalities tend to stress their cultural ties to central and western Europe and may even look down on the supposedly less civilized Russians.

Soviet society thus is a jumble of languages, races, and cultures. The task of making one nation out of them, or even of keeping this mixed society functioning, is complicated by the fact that the feelings of these various component peoples toward each other have not always been friendly. A long tradition of hostility, in fact, has sown suspicion between Georgians and Armenians, between Muslims and Jews. Some of the Soviet nations, as we have seen, especially in the Baltic and Transcaucasus areas, have in the past nursed feelings of superiority over the Russians, and hence a resentment at being ruled by them. Even where such feelings of superiority did not exist, the policies of discrimination and russification pursued by

* Counting every minor tribe, Soviet statistics in 1917 listed 182 separate nationalities speaking 149 different languages as living on Soviet territory.

tsarist governments in the last decades before the revolution promoted resentment and hatred among Russia's national minorities. Once aroused, such feelings may linger on for decades and may today be factors still to reckon with.

The multi-national composition of Soviet society has therefore always presented problems to the government of the USSR and to the Communist party which fomulates its policies. The party seized power in 1917 with a conflicting set of objectives regarding the national minorities. On the one hand, the Communists had sought to gain followers among Russia's subject nationalities by resolutely defending (though not advocating) the break-up of the tsarist empire: the rather Wilsonian slogan of "national self-determination" therefore was part of the Communist platform. On the other hand, this liberal aim was qualified by very strong reservations. The Communist leadership wished to keep the former Russian empire together as much as possible; far from favoring decentralization, federalism, or any kind of national autonomy, even if only in the cultural realm, they believed in strict centralization, presumably based on the international solidarity of all workers and toilers. To complicate matters further, the party harbored many members and leaders who sharply disagreed with Lenin's liberal slogan or his centralist predilections, or both.*

In practice, circumstances, including the dictates of geography and the fortunes of war, forced a compromise

---

* The resolution of these conflicts was made more difficult because of considerable ambiguities in the views of Marx and Engels concerning nationalism and national minorities. See Solomon F. Bloom, *The World of Nations* (New York, 1941).

on the Soviet regime. As a result of the revolution and subsequent civil war, Poland, Finland, and the Baltic states made themselves independent of Russia altogether. Georgia, Armenia and, to some extent, the Muslim principalities of central Asia, enjoyed brief periods of autonomy or independence, but were re-conquered and incorporated in the Soviet state in the early years after the revolution. A similar fate befell, some twenty years later, the Baltic provinces and portions of Poland and Rumania. The resulting political structure was given the shape of a federal union comprising today fifteen Soviet Socialist Republics of widely divergent area and population. According to the Soviet Constitution, these constituent republics are endowed with sovereignty. Their rights include that of conducting foreign relations with other governments, maintaining their own armed forces, and seceding from the federal union. These rights are largely inoperative; the exercise of some of them is regarded as illegal; the sovereignty of the republics is so thoroughly limited by the superior authority of the federal union that we must dismiss it as meaningless. So also is the supposed autonomy of various "autonomous" republics, regions, and provinces which are not full-fledged Union Republics. What autonomy remains is the right to administer certain matters of local concern and to use the language of the dominant national minority in all official business, including court trials and schooling.

One other major element of the compromise effected after the empire had been gathered together was the promotion of cultural autonomy in minority areas—precisely the policy which before the revolution the Bolsheviks had repudiated. This consisted in the vigorous encouragement of the various minorities to use their languages and to cultivate their national heritage in art, literature, history, folklore, and customs. The Communist regime adopted and pursued this policy of cultural decentralization in a period when its dictatorship was comparatively lax, and when, in addressing social problems, it experimented with a variety of solutions which might be labeled avant-guardist, progressive, or libertarian. Once, however, the government embarked on its ambitious crash program of industrialization, avant-guardist experiments and easy-going relationships became dysfunctional, and cultural autonomy henceforth was severely curbed. Although never clearly repudiated, it was reinterpreted so as to suppress any views or practices likely to jeopardize administrative centralization and the pursuit of over-all national objectives. The entire nation's culture was now to be "socialist in content, and national in form," to use the regime's own phrase.

Behind this phrase, we may detect a number of subsidiary views and objectives. The central goal which overrides all others is that of industrialization and urbanization. It implies the intention to co-ordinate all of the nation's activities by central plans for the purpose of bringing the machine age, the city, and its way of life to all corners of the country. Of necessity, this implies a profound hostility to all aspects of national culture which do not fit in with the regime's conception of modern life, of industrialism, and of socialism. Perhaps we can add to this some reference to the galloping bureaucratization of life in the Soviet Union and the rise to power and authority of people with a bureaucratic frame of mind—organization men and authoritarian personalities who tend to be suspicious of all heterogeneity and are unable or unwilling to cope with it, except by annihilating or suppressing all those people who do not fit their own stereotype of normal citizens. Such an unfocused intolerance is different from popular prejudice against specific nationalities, such as certain widely held antagonisms against Jews, Armenians, and Gypsies. Western scholars have often felt that, on occasion, the Soviet regime has manifested some readiness to cater even to such latent feelings of discrimination, or to give in to them in structuring educational opportunities and career lines. Yet these discriminatory inclinations have not expressed themselves in the allocation of housing, in resort facilities, or in social life. The average Soviet citizen does not seem to have strongly developed racial prejudices, and the Great-Russians do not show any feelings of national superiority over other Soviet citizens. Under Stalin, they were proclaimed to be the country's leading nationality; and I have at times been tempted to say that in Soviet society the Great-Russian was in a fashion the equivalent of our white Protestant Anglo-Saxon—more equal than others in a society of equals, or slightly favored in any competition with otherwise similarly endowed citizens. There is not sufficient evidence, however, to back up this impression.

To the extent that national consciousness presents a threat to the political integrity of the Soviet state, the party seeks, naturally, to curb or neutralize it. At the same time, there have been occasions when the regime seems to have promoted nationalism so as to pit various minorities against each other, in the manner of the slogan, *divide et impera.* For instance, in central Asia, a relatively homogeneous native population was divided into several nationalities, each with its own union republic and language, with the obvious aim of weakening pan-Turanian tendencies prevalent in this region. Moreover, the promotion of national consciousness and separateness has at times given the Kremlin minor advantages in its dealings with other nations of the world. Still, by and large, I would agree with Hugh Seton-Watson when he says that the Soviet regime's long-range aim is a "war of extermination against the principle of nationality."[1] The Communist party wishes to weld Soviet society into a more homogeneous whole and seeks to make its country into a thoroughly effective melting pot of nationalities. The party platform adopted in 1961 makes this fairly clear:

> Attaching decisive importance to the development of the socialist content of the cultures of the peoples of the U.S.S.R., the Party will promote their further mutual enrichment and *rapprochement,* the consolidation of their international basis, and thereby the formation of the future single world-wide culture of communist society. While supporting the progressive traditions of each people, and making them the property of all Soviet people, the Party will in all ways further new revolutionary traditions of the builders of communism common to all nations.[2]

Again, this urge for social homogeneity can be understood most easily as part of the country's industrialization drive. The central planning which this drive necessitates calls for the curbing of regional autonomy. The tasks of administering a large and complex industrial society require that all citizens understand each other; hence to homogenize the country means to russify it, at least to a degree. Most of all, however, industrialization requires a population which is attuned in its very habits and outlook to the way of life of the machine age. It therefore demands the neutralization of pre-industrial patterns of living; and these are intimately related to national peculiarities and traditions.

This is particularly evident when we realize that religion is part and parcel of virtually every national culture. Hence hostility against one implies hostility to the other. To promote national culture while combating religion means to promote national culture very selectively, and with considerable ambivalence.

The anti-religious bias of the Soviet regime is explained in part by the heritage of Marxist philosophy with its dogmatic atheism. Among the Russian Communists, this was reinforced by the fact that, historically, religious institutions were associated with political reaction and counter-revolution. The churches were part of the old order which was to be swept away. The attempts which the regime made in the 1920's to destroy religious organizations by jailing the clergy, closing down houses of worship, confiscating church funds and treasures, and persecuting believers, were based on this deeply ingrained antagonism to all organized religion. More recent attempts to destroy or harass the churches were undoubtedly reinforced by the realization that religious practices interfere with the industrialization effort and with the Soviet way of life in general. For one thing, religious practices interfere with daily work. Religious holidays constitute a disruption of the citizens' duties. Fasting weakens their efficiency. Regular prayers mean time-out from work. Many religious practices of Buddhists, Muslims, Jews, and others, may be contrary to the commands of modern medical knowledge and hygiene. Religious food taboos and other dietary practices interfere with the regime's food distribution system; any special consideration given to religious believers thus threatens the efficiency of the political and economic bureaucracy. Furthermore, religious law may come into conflict with Soviet law; and in such a clash the party can hardly be expected to make concessions. Religious law therefore must be outlawed. And what I have said about religious laws and traditions applies, more generally, to national traditions and the entire national way of life, religious or secular.

Once all this has been said, we must be aware that three decades or more of struggling against religions has not eliminated religious practices among the various national minorities any more than among the Great-Russian majority. Broad strata among Soviet Russia's Muslims, Buddhists, and other non-Russian faiths seem to carry on at least part of their traditional rituals, adapting their practices to the prevailing pattern of Soviet life and to the degree of grudging tolerance shown by the Communist party.

The same can be said for the preservation of national culture and customs in general. Those utterly out of tune with the Soviet ways of life tend to disappear. Those that can be tolerated or adapted tend to maintain themselves and to be cultivated, with many nationalities apparently clinging fervently to those of their own behavior traits which they are allowed to keep. This is true of national costumes as well as living habits. It applies to the careful cultivation of national or folk traditions in art, music, literature, and history. All these elements of national culture are promoted to the extent that they do not conflict with the Soviet way of life. This means, among other things, the elimination of the religious element from art and the careful falsification of history, or, as the Communist party platform of 1961 puts it, it opposes any "idealization of the past and the veiling of social contradictions in the history of the peoples."

How significant a concession to national culture this is remains controversial. On the one hand, the imposition of standardized Soviet patterns of life has meant the destruction of national cultures as they previously existed. Settling nomads on collective farms, converting Gypsies into factory workers, or eliminating private trade in Armenia or southern central Asia so thoroughly changes the way of life of the people affected that their very identity and survival are threatened. If, nonetheless, the external trappings of their old national culture are preserved and cultivated, this could mean that they have become stage props in the manner in which hillbilly music and cowboy craftsmanship in our culture have become stage props. We view them during leisure hours for our amusement and, perhaps, for the purpose of nostalgically transporting ourselves into a preindustrial setting. This would imply that members of the national minorities ought to be regarded as Soviet citizens in national garb, just as some people would define the people of contemporary Japan as kimono-clad Westerners.

On the other hand, there are indications that national differences persist and are deepening, so that the minorities in various areas are in fact remaining distinct nations with no more than a superficial Soviet varnish. Again, some observers would similarly say about contemporary Japan that it has remained a distinct national culture with but a thin coating of Western living patterns. The conflict between these two views is not merely a dry academic exercise. On the contrary, it expresses a difficult problem of great interest to contemporary social science—namely, the question of how much weight to assign to the persistence of different cultural traditions against the homogenizing influence of modern industrialism.

One long-range development in the Soviet Union, to which we have alluded already, seems likely to undermine the persistency of national culture patterns. This is the trend toward russification. It takes several forms in the USSR. One of these might be called colonization; and by this I mean the movement of Russians or, more generally, Slavs and other non-natives, into areas predominantly inhabited by some minority. This process has taken place so rapidly in some parts of the country, that in certain union republics the native population is today outnumbered by Russians. This appears to be the case in Kazakhstan, as well as in the western portions of the Ukrainian and Bielorussian republics, possibly also in Moldavia, Mongolia, Sakhalin, and the Kurile Islands. Another aspect of russification is the widespread use of the Russian language and its imposition as the second language all school children are expected to learn. To be sure, primary schools and many higher educational institutions conduct their classes in the language of the dominant minority; and the native tongue may be used in all official business within each union republic. Nonetheless, a person unfamiliar with Russian will be handicapped, because many schools, public institutions, and places of work have mixed clienteles; and in such cases Russian becomes the lingua franca. Its exclusive use in such agencies as the armed forces promotes this development further. In many subtle ways, through new vocabulary and the use of the Cyrillic alphabet, even the minority languages themselves are in a slow process of russification.

One might argue further that the weight of the Russian Communist party and the Russian republic within the entire political system are so overwhelming, and that this system is so tightly centralized, that in effect the national minorities are politically subordinate to the Russians. More specifically, Russian supremacy even in minority areas is secured by the policy of assigning Russians (or at least non-natives) to some of the most important positions of authority in the several union republics. The fact that the First Secretary of republican and provincial party organizations in central Asia usually is a native, while the Second Secretary is a Russian, Ukrainian, or Georgian, might be interpreted by skeptical observers as an indication that the First Secretaryship in these areas is a ceremonial office, and that decisive control resides with the Second Secretary.

The summary of methods by which russification or at least control is achieved remains incomplete unless we call attention to the regime's readiness to use naked force in imposing its will on the national minorities. I have already mentioned the violent methods used in trying to destroy organized religion. Of course, the same methods were applied against the Russians themselves; but perhaps their impact on the national minorities may have been more traumatic. Similarly, the years 1936–38 were a period in which an entire generation of civic leaders was decimated in the so-called Great Purge. Here, too, the police terror seems to have made a cleaner sweep of the national elites than it did of the Russian. The Great Purge appears to have been far more savage in central Asia and the Ukraine than in other areas of the USSR. In later years, too, selected nationalities were subjected to sweeping punitive or preventive police methods which at times differed little from actual genocide. Entire nationalities suspected of widespread disloyalty to the Soviet regime were wiped out during and after World War II; and mass deportations to labor camps or remote regions decimated the ranks of the people in areas added to the Soviet Union in the 1940's.

Instead of speaking about the resultant tendencies as russification, one might return to the image of the melting pot. All the policies enumerated above seem to weaken the cohesion and strength of the national minorities, if only because the Soviet system dilutes the purity of minority populations. The homogenizing process is speeded up by the sheer physical scrambling-up of the nationalities. Not only do Russians colonize the minority areas; the minorities in their turn are also on the move. Their educated members are mobile because the party or the government may assign them to posts all over the USSR. Common work and common schooling integrate people from all nationalities. So does military service; and so, finally, do the forced-labor camps.

Having noted the many factors contributing to the Soviet melting pot, let me list some countervailing tendencies. One of these is the remarkable tenacity with which some of the minority peoples cling to cultural patterns not in conflict with the Soviet way of life. We have already mentioned this strength of national culture. While it may be a clinging to externals, it is matched by the pronounced clannishness which many minorities exhibit. Social contacts between natives and non-natives are infrequent in many minority areas. A cultural gap is maintained by both. Intermarriage in some of these areas is the exception. In central Asia, for instance, intermarriage between Muslims and Christians makes the young couple outcasts in both parent communities.[3]

The persistence of such cultural gaps has been acknowledged by the Communist party leadership. In the 1961 party platform they declared: "The obliteration of national distinctions, and especially of language distinctions, is a considerably longer process than the obliteration of class distinctions."

Turning to the educated elites among the minorities, we confront a highly complex attitude. To some extent, they are likely to be uprooted and alienated from their own societies, without necessarily being integrated into Russian culture. Instead, we can expect them to be thoroughly acculturated to both twentieth-century civilization and to over-all Soviet behavior patterns. Many of them will be torn between the desire to assimilate and their loyalty to their own native culture. Richard Pipes, in the article just referred to, sees them as mediators between the minorities and the regime—a thankless and difficult role. My own conversations with a few educated Soviet citizens from central Asia and the Baltic republics have given me glimpses into a very ambivalent attitude, in which genuine gratitude to the Soviet regime (for its educational opportunities and career possibilities) was mixed with bitter resentment of purges and deportations which wiped out entire generations of friends and relatives. These feelings were tied together by a fierce pride in the cultural progress made by their own nationality.

What then is the total effect of Soviet nationality policies? Obviously, it too is ambiguous. Melting-pot trends in the direction of the development of a new Soviet nationality are matched by the intensification of national consciousness, if not among all the country's nationalities, then certainly among some of them. The differentiation and centrifugal tendencies resulting from this growth of national consciousness are sufficiently strong that in recent years even some high-ranking party leaders have wondered aloud whether national differences will disappear even under full-fledged communism.[4]

Soviet nationality policy has at times been compared with colonialism because the regime's relation to its minorities has involved conquest, domination, and exploitation. Unlike most other colonial countries, however, Soviet rule has sought to bring its minority subjects into the twentieth century. It has acted as an agent of Western civilization. In the short run, this is likely to promote the development of national consciousness and thus further strain the fabric of Soviet society. If, in the long run, a new Soviet nationality emerges, the Soviet variant of colonialism may be of a self-liquidating kind.

IV

Nationalism in South Africa

by

AMRY VANDENBOSCH

Nationalism in South Africa

In his challenging speech to the Parliament of South Africa on February 3, 1960, Prime Minister Harold Macmillan declared ". . . here in Africa you have yourselves created a full nation—a new nation. Indeed, in the history of our times yours will be recorded as the first of the African nationalisms." This statement raises a number of perplexing questions. What is this nation to which the British Prime Minister referred? What people constitute this nation? Macmillan probably had the Afrikaner people in mind, but do they constitute a nation? Is there a nation in South Africa, or are there several nations? Are the different peoples in the country gradually merging into a single nation?

The population of the Republic of South Africa is composed of a number of sharply divided racial and ethnic groups. Africans or Bantus constitute the largest racial group, with about two-thirds of the population.* They are divided into a number of tribes, of which the Xhoses, Zulus, and Sothos are the largest. The whites account for only about one-fifth of the population and they are far from united. The coloreds (mixed) constitute roughly one-

* The population of South Africa according to the 1960 census was divided as follows: Africans 10,807,809; whites 3,067,638; coloreds 1,488,-267; Asians 477,414; Total 15,841,128.

tenth of the total population, while Asians, chiefly Indians, account for about three per cent. To complete the picture of the complicated population structure, mention should be made of the Jewish community, which numbers about 100,000. While the Jewish people are a part of the white society, they nevertheless form a rather distinct community within it.

Bantu Nationalism

It is difficult to determine the mind of the Bantu world of South Africa with respect to nationalism. The Bantus constitute by far the largest racial group in the country, yet theirs is not the dominant nationalism, at least not yet. They have been given so little opportunity to express themselves, to develop culturally, or to engage in political activities that their nationalism has been retarded, driven underground, and perverted. It has not been permitted to enjoy a natural growth. Indeed, all political activities by Bantus are ruthlessly repressed by the government.

As early as 1912 the African National Congress was organized for the purpose of promoting and defending the interests of the Bantus in the newly formed Union of South Africa. Reflecting its membership, which was drawn from the professional class then emerging, the Congress was moderate in its demands and methods. Its aim has been not a black but a multi-racial South Africa. Chief Albert John Luthuli, Nobel Prize winner in 1961, was for some time its head. Though it became more militant in its last few years, it could no longer satisfy all of its followers. Its "young Turks" broke off to form the Pan-Africanist Congress, which in 1960 launched a campaign against the pass laws. Planned to be nonviolent, the campaign nevertheless led to serious disturbances throughout the country, ending in tragedy at Sharpeville and Langa. The government declared a national emergency which lasted for five months. Both the African National Congress and the Pan-Africanist Congress were declared unlawful, and thus banned. A number of political leaders left the country and established a South-African United Front with representatives in important centers such as London, New York, Cairo, Accra, and Dar es Salaam.

There is now no legal organization to speak for Bantu nationalism in South Africa. There are, however, secret organizations carrying on the struggle, with names like Spear of the Nation and National Liberation Movement. At the moment an underground organization, generally known as Poqo, is carrying on a campaign of antigovernment sabotage and terrorism. This movement is apparently causing the government grave concern. Minister of Justice Vorster has asserted that Poqo seeks to overthrow the government by revolution. To meet the threat he is asking Parliament for new emergency laws to deal with the situation.

For over two decades the Africans enjoyed a small, indirect representation in Parliament. In 1936 the Bantus throughout the country were granted the right to elect four senators, but they could elect only whites, since only members of this race are constitutionally qualified to serve in Parliament. The Bantus in Cape Colony were also permitted to vote for three whites to represent them in the lower house of the national parliament. When in 1959 the government announced its policy of separate development, or territorial segregation, it obtained legislation abolishing this African representation. In exchange for this type of representation in the national parliament and the Cape provincial legislative body, the Bantus are to receive political rights in a tribal governmental structure in their "homelands," the Bantustans, now being created. This can give little satisfaction to the detribalized Bantus who have lived for years, some all of their lives, in urban areas. To give people the right to vote where they do not live, and to deny them suffrage where they do live and make their living, is an anomaly and can satisfy nobody. This effort to sterilize politically the millions of Bantus in the great urban areas may well drive them toward Pan-Africanism and large-scale terrorism.

The Africans have every incentive to become strongly nationalistic, for they are subject to grievous handicaps under the white-dominated government. The pass laws drastically restrict their freedom of movement, and the right to sell their labor, and also interfere with their family life. Africans are further handicapped in pressing for higher wages, for their freedom of organization is sharply limited. Innumerable laws and regulations impose segregation in every aspect of life. Africans have been denied nearly every means of expressing their dissatisfaction. Their parliamentary representation has been abolished; their political organizations outlawed; their leaders hounded out of the country, restricted, muzzled, and jailed. It is quite natural that the politically conscious Africans should espouse Bantu nationalism as the only hope for deliverance from the semislavery in which they find themselves. The intransigence of the whites and especially of the Nationalist government is driving the

Africans into an anti-white, anti-Western and anti-missionary mood. The Bantus have begun to write and interpret their history, and as might be expected, African historians are interpreting their past in terms of a struggle against exploitation, oppression, and domination by the white man.[1] White nationalism is provoking a bitter, violent, black nationalism.

Under the circumstances it would seem that Bantu nationalism would easily win the day among Africans in South Africa. Yet a greatly respected leader, Chief Albert John Luthuli, flatly rejects it. In his book, *Let My People Go,* published in 1962, he wrote:

Who owns South Africa?
With the exception of a small group of black nationalists who have learned their politics from Dr. Verwoerd's and General Smuts' parties, *the great majority of Africans* [italics in the original] reply that the country now belongs to fourteen million people of different races—it is jointly owned by all its inhabitants, quite regardless of their color. This view, which I adhere to without qualification, demands that people be regarded primarily as people. As far as culture and habits of life are concerned, they may differ as radically as they wish. But when it comes to participation in ownership and government, race must be made wholly irrelevant.[2]

Unfortunately, most whites, and not alone the Nationalists, reject the idea of a multi-racial state. They are convinced that enfranchising persons regardless of race will speedily mean black domination, and this they are determined to prevent. Under the circumstances it would not be surprising if Luthuli no longer represents the views of the majority of his fellow-Africans and that he will be soon swept aside, if he has not already been, by more radical leaders who embrace Bantu nationalism.

At long last the whites of South Africa, including most Afrikaners, have come to recognize the existence of African nationalism and that it can no longer be suppressed. They realize that this must mean the end of white supremacy unless the two races can be geographically separated and the Africans are allowed to develop their own political life. This is the policy which the Nationalist government announced a few years ago and which it is now trying to carry out. The blacks are to be pressed back into their reserves or "homelands." These Bantustans, as they are called, are to be industrialized and allowed an increasing autonomy, and ultimately they are to be granted independence, if they desire it.[3] By this "solution" the Nationalists hope to maintain white control over the large urban and industrial areas and be freed from the adverse moral judgment of the world and the mounting pressure from the new African states.

That this bold plan can be implemented seems doubtful. The government admits that the economy of the white areas will require the presence of several million Africans for an indefinite future, but that they are to be regarded as migrants without political rights. Moreover the "migrant" Africans in the white territory are to be subject to the segregation laws which apply to them now. It is wholly unlikely that bordering independent Bantustans will be indifferent to that kind of treatment of its nationals. Continued segregation is more likely to inflame African nationalism. Southern Rhodesia is certain to have an African-controlled government before long, and when this happens Pan-African pressure will be right on South Africa's border. It is much too late for any drastic attempt by the white minority to control and direct this explosive force into channels favorable to its interests.

Afrikaner Nationalism

A distinguished South African editor has asserted that there are no South Africans, that the term has "no significance except outside South Africa, and only there because of a widespread ignorance."[4] The meaning of this situation is explained by a further statement that "if there are no South Africans, pure and simple, there are many 'qualified South Africans.' " Whatever may be the views of others on this matter, most Afrikaners are certain that they constitute the authentic South African nation. And it must be conceded at once that the Afrikaners as a people possess most of the earmarks which are generally associated with nationalism. A separate language, a distinct culture, a unity reinforced by strong religious and ecclesiastical ties, a history of struggle for the preservation of their culture and for political independence, set the Afrikaners apart from their neighbors as a distinct people.

Most of the Afrikaners of today are the descendants of a few hundred families settled by the Dutch East India Company at the Cape in 1652 and during the following half-century. The original colonists were Dutch, but in 1688 about two hundred Huguenots arrived. They were one in religion with the earlier Dutch settlers and were soon culturally absorbed. Ethnologically the Afrikaners

77

of today are predominantly Dutch, with a considerable mixture of French and some German.

Genesis and Progress of Afrikaner Nationalism

These early settlers soon began to display the characteristics which became so pronounced among the later Afrikaners. The East-India Company had established the colony at the Cape as a victualing station for its ships on the long voyage to the Indies. It wanted to keep the settlers near Cape Town to produce and deliver provisions to the ships at the lowest cost. But the settlers very early began to spread out and move beyond the control of the company's officials, to areas where they became cattle farmers. There they developed the characteristics of the frontiersmen. They became strongly individualistic. Conditions of life were hard and could be endured only by hardened men.

It is in these treks, as the Boers called them, that the genesis of Afrikaner nationalism is to be found. As the Afrikaners moved east and north they encountered Bantu tribes coming down from the north. Unlike the Indian tribes which American Western frontiersmen met, the Bantus were too numerous to be exterminated or pushed back. They were subordinated socially and economically. There developed the complex of master-subject relationships which much later came to be called apartheid. The Boers were hostile to governmental authority because it challenged their attitudes and values. This was especially true after 1815, when the British replaced the Dutch as the rulers of Cape Colony. The trekkers (pioneers) strongly resented the British policy of protecting the

Bantus from some of the harsh practices of the Boers. The frontiersmen likewise resented the missionaries, and for much the same reason. Missionaries sympathized with the Bantus and had equalitarian ideas.

During the years 1836–54 there occurred what is known in South African history as the Great Trek. In a sense it was merely the continuation of the migration from the Cape Town area to the frontier regions which had been going on throughout the eighteenth century and into the early years of the nineteenth century, but it was planned and organized and on a larger scale. There were several causes for the Great Trek. The Voortrekkers (first group of pioneers) complained that the government was not providing the frontier regions with security; it failed to protect them from raids by the Bantu tribes. But the main cause was the policy of the British government toward the Bantus and the coloreds. Interesting in this connection is the statement by Anna Steenkamp, a niece of one of the leaders of the movement, because it throws much light on the prejudices of the Voortrekkers:

> The shameful and unjust proceedings with reference to the freedom of our slaves; and yet it is not so much their freedom which drove us to such lengths, as their being placed on an equal footing with Christians, contrary to the laws of God, and the natural distinction of race and color, so that it was intolerable for any decent Christian to bow down beneath such a yoke, wherefore we rather withdrew in order thus to preserve our doctrines in purity.[5]

It has been suggested that the Voortrekkers moved on not so much because of hatred of the British rule as a dislike of all government. There was much division among

79

them. In the northern territories they set up many small states, which often quarreled and fought among themselves. They established the Republic of Natal with the seat of government at Pietermaritzburg, but constant hostilities with the Zulus weakened it so much that it was about to fall apart. The British annexed it in 1843. In the north two states finally emerged, the Orange Free State and the South African Republic, commonly known as the Transvaal. The Boer republics were constantly under British pressure. With the discovery of gold and diamonds in their territories and the large-scale invasion of English and others which followed, the doom of the agrarian republics was sealed. But they did not go under without a heroic fight which held a mighty empire at bay and won the applause of the world.*

The defeat of the Boer republics and their extinction as independent states did not mean the defeat of Afrikaner nationalism. Quite the reverse, it intensified Afrikaner nationalism and set the stage for its final triumph. A bitter imperialistic war was followed by a magnanimous peace. The former Boer republics were soon granted self-government, and a little later the two ex-republics and the two British dependencies, Natal and Cape Colony, became politically unified. The governments of the Union from 1910 to 1948 represented a fusion of English and Afrikaners but in the latter year the Nationalist (Afrikaner) party won the victory at the polls. It has been in power ever since. Under it, all of the goals and ideals of Afrikaner nationalism have been realized. The Afrikaans

* The Boer War, or the Second Anglo-Boer War (1899–1902), called by Afrikaners the Second War for Independence, the first having occurred in 1881.

culture and language have been granted full equality, the Boer racial policy has been extended and enforced by innumerable laws, and the goals of complete national independence and republicanism were achieved in 1961, when the Union became a republic. For full measure it also withdrew from the Commonwealth.*

* Actual independence had been won long before the Nationalists came to power, and membership in the Commonwealth involved no restrictions on South African sovereignty, but extreme nationalists wanted to get rid of everything which reminded them of earlier British control.

Elements in Afrikaner Nationalism[6]

Language and church are probably the chief cohesive forces of the Afrikaners. General Smuts once described Afrikaans as Dutch with the grammar dropped out.† This is an apt if over-simple description, for this language is more than phonetic Dutch or a Dutch patois. It is sometimes asserted that Afrikaans was a political innovation but this is an exaggeration. Under the conditions prevailing in South Africa, especially the cultural isolation, high Dutch was bound to break down. For a long period the Afrikaners spoke one language and wrote another. It is remarkable how long high Dutch continued to be the language of polite society, the church, the government, and even of politics,‡ but after a time Afrikaners became weary of speaking one language and writing another. The first book in Afrikaans was published in 1861 and the

† In a conversation with the writer in 1945.

‡ For example, as late as 1918, Dr. D. F. Malan, the Nationalist leader, made an important political speech in Dutch; *De Onafhankelikheid van Zuid-Afrika* was given at Malmesbury August 31, 1918 (Cape Town, 1918).

second twelve years later. The first Afrikaans Bible was published in 1933 and the psalms and hymns in Afrikaans were first used in Dutch Reformed churches in 1944. An Afrikaans literature has been steadily building up but is still not extensive. Its poetry is unique and of a high quality.

The South African Dutch Reformed churches have been described as the Nationalist party at prayer. This thrust is unfair to these churches, yet it contains a significant element of truth. In the rural regions "volk" and "kerk" are closely identified. The churches constituted very nearly the only civilizing influence in the frontier regions. The Dutch Reformed churches and Afrikaner nationalism have been closely associated. The Afrikaners were and are a deeply religious people. The heroic President Paul Kruger of the Transvaal and President Burger of the Orange Free State were ministers of the church; Dr. D. F. Malan, Prime Minister of the Union from 1948 to 1955, left the pastorate to become a Nationalist editor and leader. More than any other Christian bodies in South Africa, the Dutch Reformed churches have supported nationalist policies. In recent years, however, there is discernible an increasing reluctance to endorse or to give tacit consent, and steadily more church leaders denounce apartheid as incompatible with Christianity.[7]

An aspect of the experience of the trekkers and their interpretation of it gave Afrikaner nationalism an unlovely character. They saw a marked similarity between their experience and that of the ancient Hebrews who were led by God out of the house of bondage into the land of Canaan, where they had to conquer a homeland from the pagan peoples who dwelt there. So the Boers had been called by God out of the house of British bondage to open up the interior for civilization and the propagation of the Christian gospel among the inferior heathen who dwelt in the land. They developed a strong sense of divine national calling and destiny. Under the circumstances it is not strange that they also developed a self-righteous attitude.

English and Afrikaner historians hold strikingly different views of the Great Trek. Many of the former regard it as the great disaster of South African history. It retarded the development of Cape Colony and destroyed South Africa's national unity, caused tension and finally war between Boer and Briton, and bitterly divided the two white races instead of uniting them. Had Cape Colony gradually pushed out its borders all these misfortunes would have been avoided.[8] Afrikaners, on the other hand, regard the Great Trek as the most glorious page of their national history and from it draw patriotic fervor. The centennial celebration of this movement in 1938 was turned into a rollicking holiday of Afrikaner nationalism. They feel that if there had been no Great Trek and Cape Colony had expanded, the Boers would have been absorbed into the British nation. It was in the Great Trek that the Afrikaner nation was born.

The Afrikaners feared the loss of their own peculiar culture. When sovereignty was transferred to the British after the Napoleonic wars, they were convinced that an attempt would be made to Anglicize them. This intensified their consciousness of being a distinct people. When English was made the official language and Scotch ministers were imported to fill vacant Dutch Reformed pulpits, they were sure their fears had been confirmed. They reacted by closing ranks in defense of their culture. The

83

fear of Anglicization was again aroused after the conquest of the Boer republics. The Afrikaners believed that the main object of the policy of Lord Milner, the British High Commissioner, was the extermination of the Boer way of life and the absorption of the Boers into the British nation. On the other hand, Lord Milner had his suspicions of Boer intentions. Toward the end of the war he wrote: "There is no doubt whatever in my mind that the Dutch will try, for a time at least, to recover by politics what they have lost by arms."[9]

Milner's apprehensions proved soundly based. By politics the Afrikaners recovered far more than they lost in 1902. In less than fifty years they had acquired complete political control over all of South Africa—the two former British colonies of Natal and the Cape as well as the territories of the former republics—and achieved complete political independence from London. A dozen years more and they had achieved their cherished ideal of republicanism by abolishing the monarchy.

This fear of absorption through Anglicization also caused a core of Afrikaners to oppose the fusionist policies of Botha and Smuts. They feared that the policy of conciliation advocated and followed by the two former Boer generals would inevitably lead to absorption of the Afrikaners into the British nation. When Botha and Smuts loyally supported the British in World War I they were denounced as traitors to "het volk," and they had the painful task of suppressing a rebellion of irreconcilable Boers. The bitterness caused by the use of force against fellow Boers had a profound influence on the development of Afrikaner nationalism.

It is difficult to escape the conclusion that social and

economic causes were also strongly influential in the development of Afrikaner nationalism. The Boers were agrarian and many of them were very poor. The so-called "poor whites" numbered about 20 per cent of the white population and most of them were Boers. The British controlled finance, commerce, industry, and the government. The Afrikaners held a secondary position in nearly every phase of life. There thus developed an anti-British, anti-capitalist, anti-imperialist spirit. After the formation of the Union, the Afrikaner's numerical superiority gave him a political advantage over the English-speaking South Africans. He used this political power not only to obtain a status of equality for his culture, but also to improve his economic and social position. This anti-capitalist, anti-imperialist spirit still occasionally finds expression from high government officials. Albert Hertzog, a member of the present cabinet and son of the former Boer general and Union Prime Minister, in 1962 accused American international finance of seeking to wipe out the whites in South Africa, of making possible a black take-over, and of breaking South Africa spiritually by destroying the white man's pride.[10] Many Afrikaner nationalists were attracted by national socialism, though they generally added the prefix Christian. Former Prime Minister Hertzog declared in 1941 that "Liberal capitalism was responsible for the destruction of the Boer Republics, and the impoverishment of all Germany."[11] He is said to have been completely converted to a South African national socialism based on Portuguese doctrines.[12] The Ossewabrandwag, a semisecret organization which flourished during World War II years, displayed nationalist-socialist sympathies and fascist tactics.

Indians and Coloreds and Nationalism

In its racial policy the Nationalist Party finds it difficult to accord anything like a reasonable role to the coloreds and the Indians. For a long time it was hoped that by pressure and financial aid the Indians could be induced to return to their country of origin. Most whites have given up the idea of repatriation as a solution to the Indian problem, though some Nationalist leaders seem still to hold this out as a hope.[13] The Indians find themselves in a very uncomfortable position. Diplomatic pressure on South Africa by India has won them little; a strenuous South African Indian nationalism would almost certainly be met by more discrimination and repression. Indians fear African domination almost as much as do the whites. If accorded political rights and fairer treatment the Indians would very probably support the Nationalist government on many measures. The Nationalist leaders argue that if political rights were accorded Indians the right of suffrage could not be denied the Bantus, and this they are determined at all costs not to do. The prospect for the Indian community is an unhappy one.

The problem of what to do with the coloreds causes most Nationalists great distress. The coloreds share with the whites a common culture; large numbers of them speak Afrikaans and are members of the Dutch Reformed churches. No responsible Nationalist has ever suggested territorial segregation for this group. Until World War II it was assumed that they would be politically integrated into the European society. It was believed that any other policy would be both unjust and unwise.[14] The addition of a million and a half coloreds to the white community would greatly strengthen it; their defection to the Africans would greatly weaken it. Nevertheless, the present government has sternly set its face against any measures which look toward their assimilation with the whites. It adamantly opposes giving the coloreds representation by their own people, even on a separate electoral roll, on the ground that any concession of political rights to the coloreds would undermine the logic of denying the same rights to Indians and Africans.[15]

Many Nationalists are unhappy about this policy. *Die Burger,* the Nationalist daily newspaper of Cape Town, which represents the view of this section of the party, declared:

> Those people who are favorably disposed towards direct representation of the coloreds are in the minority in the ranks of the Afrikaners but they are not few in numbers nor are they insignificant. Some of them have come to adopt their standpoint after much struggle, some through prayer as well.[16]

What effect is this rejection having on the attitude of the coloreds? *Die Burger* of January 1, 1960, fears that they may, out of animosity toward the Afrikaners, deliberately Anglicize themselves. According to statements in Parliament large numbers of the colored people are becoming estranged from the Afrikaners.[17] Had they been allowed to become assimilated with the whites the coloreds would almost certainly have accepted Afrikaner nationalism. Their lot is indeed a sad one. Where will they go? Where can they go?

The coloreds and Indians present the government with a dilemma. To make its policy of refusing to grant political rights to them more palatable, to assuage troubled consciences and somewhat reduce harsh foreign criticism of this policy, the Nationalist government is spending generous sums on the education of these peoples. But this can only increase the dissatisfaction of the new and better-educated generation with a denial of basic human rights. Better education and more income can only lead to greater demands.

English-Speaking Community and Nationalism

The English in South Africa have shown no tendency or inclination toward a nationhood. Unlike the British in the thirteen colonies in North America, they were a minority, even of the whites. To prevent absorption, subordination, or subjection, they needed the support of the mother country. They wanted to remain a part of the British world-nation and to keep South Africa in some fashion a part of the British Empire or Commonwealth. The position of the Afrikaners was the reverse. They had lost political, and thereby also much cultural, contact with their mother country, Holland, a long time before. Moreover, Holland was small and its extensive overseas territories were hostages of the British Empire and its sea power. The Afrikaners, especially after the Boer War, knew they stood alone in the world, and they resented the political and cultural advantages which the English enjoyed because of their relationship with a mother-country which was a great power. The creation of the Union in 1910 united the country politically, but the division between the Afrikaners and the English was not eliminated. The fusion of the white people which was universally proclaimed at the convention which effected union was not realized. The political co-operation between the two peoples with which the Union began steadily deteriorated until in 1948 a wholly Afrikaner Nationalist government came into power.

The political impotence of the English after union strengthened their feeling of identity with the mother-country. This exposed the English-speaking people to the Afrikaner charge of not being good citizens, of being more loyal to England than South Africa, or at best having a divided loyalty. Only Afrikaners were genuine South Africans. Afrikaner Nationalists were prone to regard all English-speaking persons as either potential Afrikaners or aliens.

Toward a South African Nation?

With the advent of the Republic in 1961, the triumph of the Afrikaner Nationalists was substantially complete. Since then Prime Minister Verwoerd has put less emphasis on the pursuit of purely Afrikaner interests and more on black-white relations. The proclamation of the Republic coincided with mounting pressure on South Africa from the new African states and the world. The events in the Congo and the plight of the white settlers in the Rhodesias and in Kenya have caused great anxiety among all whites in South Africa. Nationalist leaders always contended that relations between the Afrikaners and the English would improve once the Union became a republic. After the referendum in October, 1960, which gave a two per cent majority for a republic, Verwoerd expressed the belief that in spite of the bitter campaign the conflict of nationalities had ended and that in consequence South Africans "need never again feel like two nations in one state."[18]

As internal and external pressure on South Africa increases because of its racial policy, this theme is emphasized more and more. In this critical situation the Nationalist government undoubtedly desires and feels the need of the support of all the whites. It is therefore appealing for unity among the white people. The appeal is remarkably broadened, as is evident from the following statement in Parliament by the Prime Minister on January 25, 1963:

> Amongst us white people a new relationship has been created as the result of certain . . . great deeds, great reforms, particularly constitutional reforms, and in fact a new nation is growing up. In the constitutional sphere South Africa has experienced a great change. Today nobody feels unhappy about it any longer. Everybody realizes that the establishment of the Republic of South Africa was to the benefit of the whole nation and of the growth of a new nation.

The same note was struck by President Swart at the unveiling of a monument at Graham:

> We entered a new period in the history of our country when the Republic was established last year. Everywhere we find a new spirit in our nation, especially in the descendants of the Voortrekkers on the one hand and the descendants of the British settlers on the other.
>
> I know of no other instrument which symbolizes the unity and mutual respect, bonds of friendship and communal patriotism better than this monument which I am unveiling.[19]

The appeal for unity was made in more tangible ways as well. In 1961 two English-speaking politicians were added to the Cabinet, which since 1948 had been composed exclusively of Afrikaners. Afrikaner nationalist wooing of the English is being carried on in many ways.

What is the significance of these movements? Are the Afrikaners and English co-operating merely under the stress of the racial crisis? Many English-speaking South Africans basically are in favor of the Nationalist racial policy, others reluctantly go along because as matters have developed they feel that they have no alternative. Or are the English-speaking people moving into the Nationalist camp? Since the political connection with the United Kingdom was dissolved and the measures on behalf of Afrikaner culture and nationalism entrenched beyond recall, they probably feel that continuation of the old political feud becomes senseless. One sometimes feels that while the English talk about integration they really want apartheid, and ironically, while the Nationalists have talked vociferously about apartheid they have allowed integration. Since 1948, the movement of the Bantus to the large urban areas has been allowed to continue, and that at an accelerated pace.

That many of the English will be politically absorbed is clear, but will they be culturally absorbed? Do the English-speaking Africans now have reason to fear for the survival of the English language, just as in the past Afrikaners feared the disappearance of their own culture? Are the English going to become Afrikaners? This is highly unlikely. Afrikaners in the end are more likely to be absorbed by the English. There is evidence that the Afrikaner Nationalists fear this, as is evident from stray statements made by them. In discussing the bi-lingualism of the country, Professor P. J. C. Coertze of the Afrikaans

91

University of Pretoria admitted that an amalgamation process was taking place, and added "As an Afrikaner I hope this will be an enlarged Afrikaner nation."[20]

Many Afrikaners would like to eliminate English as one of the official languages, but this is not possible. English-speaking persons have a distinct advantage in business, in industry, and in all affairs involving international contacts. Afrikaans students find themselves at a disadvantage in studying abroad. The number of good books in Afrikaans is still limited. No Afrikaner can go very far in literature, or science, or anything else if he confines himself to the publications in his native language. The Afrikaners constitute nearly 60 per cent of the white population, but practically all of the immigrants either come from the British Isles or soon adopt English as their language. The present numerical superiority of the Afrikaners over the English is no guarantee that the Afrikaner culture will remain dominant. Moreover, because Afrikaans has become identified in the African mind with apartheid, Bantus will prefer English as their national language. Africans say that when they come to power there will be one official language, and that will be English.

If one cares to hazard a prediction at this moment it would be that the English-speaking South Africans will move in considerable numbers toward Afrikaner nationalism but that culturally the movement will be from Afrikaans to English. There may emerge something like a united white South African nation.

But this cannot be the end. The future is with the Africans because of their great numerical superiority. Thus Afrikaner nationalism after its amazing triumph in its one hundred fifty years' struggle for predominance must eventually come to a dead end. It had remarkable qualities and there was much about it which compelled admiration. There is also great tragedy in many aspects of its development. It moved from oppressed to oppressive nationalism, from strong individualism to stifling group conformity, from political unification to a proposed Balkanization of the country because of its unwillingness to accept a multi-racial state, from championship of democracy to obdurate basic denial of it. Afrikaners used to call themselves "children of protest"; now the Nationalist government suppresses all protest.

V

Communism's Impact on African Nationalism

by

G. MENNEN WILLIAMS

Communism's Impact on African Nationalism

One of my significant tasks at the Department of State is to scrutinize and evaluate Communist attempts to infiltrate and subvert the efforts of the peoples of Africa to achieve their aspirations for freedom, independence, and social and economic progress. In this lecture I propose to review recent Communist bloc activities throughout that continent. There are, however, incipient opportunities for Communist penetration in the southern regions of Africa, as the forces for independence and self-government in those regions collide with the forces determined to hang on to the status quo. We are aware of such dangers and are watching them closely, and here I will examine further the question of how the southern African situation could invite Communist attention.

Two years ago, the Communists had hopes of reporting success on their party congress resolutions to penetrate Africa. But today the Communists have little to show for their not-inconsiderable efforts. Two years ago, they had a foothold in the Congo and hoped to capture the heart of Africa. Through the determination of Congolese leadership and the success of the United Nations in reuniting Katanga with the rest of the country, those hopes have been dashed. Despite heavy investment in West and North Africa, the Communists have failed to subvert African countries to their way of thinking.

While the Communists have made many mistakes and while the Free World has continued to offer Africans the alternative of freedom and progress, the main reason for Communist failures is Africa's spirit of independence. The peoples and countries of Africa guard their newly won independence jealously and refuse to submit to any ideology which seeks to fit them into an alien mold under foreign direction.

The past year, however, has also shown clearly that there is no inclination by the Communist bloc to relax its efforts in Africa. In fact, there have been continuing and diligent efforts by the Communists, despite setbacks they have encountered, to extend their influence throughout the continent. There is little effort to evangelize the Communist ideology; the chief emphasis is on power politics. The principal aim of Communist activities, at the present time and for the near future, continues to be destruction of the Western position in Africa. The Communists also want to insinuate themselves in African good graces through the establishment of an identity of Communist Bloc-African positions on major international issues. Their long-range goal, however, remains the creation of Communist governments in Africa.

The Bloc continues to press for every opportunity to widen its influence in Africa wherever and whenever it can. It has made offers of financial and arms assistance to various subversive and nationalist organizations and has attempted to foment unrest by offering to provide, or by actually providing, arms aid to countries which have, or conceivably could have, disputes with their neighbors. It continues, in spite of difficulties with African students, to encourage young Africans to attend Communist universities, thus hoping to develop future cells of Communist agents. Even if ninety out of one hundred students should backslide, the Communists hope the remaining ten will return to Africa to form Communist cells in the areas of greatest sensitivity.

In 1962, Africa continued to be a most important target for Communist bloc propaganda. There were important increases in most of the media in use—publications, radio broadcasting, films, cultural exchanges, and scholarships.

Although four pro-Communist papers were suspended in Africa last year, sixteen others had an estimated circulation of 100,000, and Communist-oriented material appeared regularly in several government-controlled newspapers. Inexpensive Communist publications sent into Africa increased their coverage of African affairs and improved their distribution channels.

Bloc broadcasts to Africa increased by approximately 50 per cent during the year, rising from about two hundred hours a week to nearly three hundred hours. Almost 20 per cent of the total broadcast time to sub-Saharan Africa was in Amharic, Hausa, Somali, and Swahili, four important indigenous languages.

Bloc production of documentary films on African subjects appears to have declined in the past year, but the number of showings of films in existence increased significantly.

Cultural agreements of various kinds with African governments rose 40 per cent in 1962, and the number of African countries involved in such agreements doubled, from seven to fourteen. Eleven countries were visited by Bloc cultural groups, and Communist athletic teams visited nine African countries.

The number of African students in Bloc institutions increased by 55 per cent over 1961, rising to a new high of some 4,700 by the end of 1962 from a previous total of about 3,000. Student disaffection, however, also rose sharply, as the Bulgarian incident has shown, and a growing number of students left the Soviet Union and other Communist countries during the year. By comparison, there are about 5,000 African students in the United States and four to five times that many in Britain and Europe. The Communists are especially active in trying to subvert African students in Europe.

The Bloc is continuing to expand its diplomatic establishment in Africa. The number of missions rose from only four in 1955 to more than eighty in 1963. The Soviets are now represented in twenty countries; the Czechs in fifteen; the Red Chinese in ten; and the Poles, the East Germans, and the Bulgarians in seven. There is also some representation in Africa of the Hungarians, the Rumanians, the Cubans, the North Koreans, and the North Vietnamese.

Moscow and the more important satellite capitals are more active in propaganda activities than Peiping because of the greater number of their missions in Africa. The long-range goals of the two giants of the Communist world are generally similar, but some differences in tactics are reflected in their approaches to still-dependent African areas. Moscow stresses "peaceful coexistence"—which means any measures short of armed conflict—and deals mainly with established governments, while Communist

China advocates violence and deals openly with any sympathetic faction within an African territory.

The increasing size of the Communist presence in Africa, together with certain Communist blunders, contributes to a heightened African awareness of the disparity between the Bloc's feigned and real objectives. There is growing recognition that Communist deeds and goals conflict with African desires to develop independently of both East and West. Communist interference in local politics, efforts to elicit African support for Bloc cold war policies, and the increased publicity given to African student problems in Bloc schools also contribute to this added awareness.

It is further reflected in the Bloc's failure in many countries to buy influence through the extension of financial credits. Only about one-sixth of the $678 million in grants and credits it has extended to African countries since 1954 has been used. Frequently the actual negotiation of these financial arrangements and the implementation of projects have engendered considerable ill will.

It is also reflected in a growing African uneasiness with Communist-front organizations, such as the Afro-Asian Peoples Solidarity Organization, which met at Moshi, Tanganyika, February, 1963. While the Communists scored some successes at Moshi, their tight control of the proceedings and their supervision of many of the delegates was disillusioning to many Africans.

As far as Communist gains were concerned, the conference increased Bloc prestige, especially among the young African nationalists who were impressed with the Communists' show of power and with the free way in which they made funds available. The conference also

101

endorsed African aspirations in various resolutions and, of course, offered increased opportunities for Communist contacts with Africans.

In spite of these gains, the Communists lost important ground for at least three reasons:

1) The conflict between Soviet and Chinese Communists could not be suppressed, and the infighting was not lost on Africans.

2) Their persistent efforts to enlarge the organization to include the Western Hemisphere showed African participants that the Communists are more interested in propaganda than in the welfare of Africa.

3) The barefaced way in which the Communists used delegates who were not really representative of African organizations or governments gave Africans firsthand evidence of the dangers of Communist intervention in Africa.

It is clear that many African governments are becoming increasingly aware of the divergence of their national interests and the aspirations of international communism. For example, the Communists made a massive effort to turn Guinea into a showplace of Bloc-development techniques and to use it as a base for the expansion of Communist influence in Africa. Bloc credits for at least $116 million were extended, and there were as many as fifteen hundred Communist technicians in Guinea. However, irregularity of deliveries, high costs, poor quality, as well as arrogant Soviet meddling in Guinean internal affairs, soon disillusioned the Guineans. At the same time, the United States presence in Guinea, with an able ambassador and country team, plus our modest aid program there, have offered a successful alternative to Sino-Soviet overtures.

In the neighboring country of Mali, African leaders have undergone a somewhat similar disillusionment and are tending toward increased confidence in the United States and the West. In Algeria, the Communist party was banned by the government only a short time after independence, and in Tunisia the Communist party was suppressed early in 1963.

Such checks to Communist aspirations in Africa do not permit any complacency on our part. Although there is reason to hope that the countries of North and West Africa will continue to develop institutions that will be increasingly immune to Communist subversion, there are still many Communist personnel throughout these areas.

Bloc strategy seems to be turning to the potentially more explosive situation in southern Africa. Here the ever-increasing demand of black Africans for self-government runs into stubborn resistance from those who cling tenaciously to minority rule. Elsewhere on the continent, the transition to independence and majority rule has generally accommodated indigenous African aspirations with European interests. But the tragic potential in large parts of southern Africa lies in the fact that there is already a profound cleavage between the Europeans— living or ruling in those areas—and the Africans. The whites seek to hold on to long-standing privileges, while the blacks will no longer passively accept a subordinate role.

It is here that the Bloc is especially watchful and seeks to feed the fires of trouble. The Communists are waiting for what they hope will be a cataclysmic struggle in which the Free World could find itself maneuvered into protecting privilege and the Communists would seem to back freedom—even though they may be actually promoting chaos in order to permit a Communist takeover. It is this strategy that endangers the position of the Free World not only in southern Africa but on the whole continent.

There are four Bloc diplomatic missions in Dar es Salaam, Tanganyika, where there are also representatives of fourteen nationalist organizations from eastern and southern Africa. It is evident that these Bloc missions are attempting to assess the relative strength and weakness of these organizations and of their leaders and the degree to which they can be influenced or used. Unless rapid political and social progress is made in these areas, the looming collision of white and black in southern Africa can open new Communist opportunities to infiltrate and influence events.

To date, Communist penetration of the southern regions of Africa has not been considerable, but the number of students from the area going to Bloc schools is rising steadily. At present, estimates indicate that there are some two hundred and fifty to three hundred students at various schools in the Bloc from the Federation of Rhodesia and Nyasaland, South Africa, the Portuguese territories and the High Commission territories. There also has been a sharp rise in the number of Africans from these areas going to the Bloc for training in guerrilla warfare and sabotage. The number of hours of Portuguese-language broadcasting from the Bloc has increased. In addition, arms are made available to various insurgent groups through independent African nations.

The Communists' principal aim in southern Africa appears to be to dominate all non-white opposition elements to the existing government in the Republic of South Africa.

Although the South African Communist party has been outlawed, it continues to exploit the tensions and frustrations generated by the government's apartheid program. The party's membership is relatively small—only an estimated eight hundred hard-core members—but it has some sixty-five hundred sympathizers. Its importance is not to be judged by its size, however, but lies in its long history of support for the African nationalist movement.

Since 1959, Communist efforts have met strong opposition from the Pan-African Congress, which, partly because of its racial outlook, has opposed the white Communist leadership and is resentful of its efforts to direct protest movements toward strengthening the Communist apparatus rather than toward the organization of a non-white nationalist movement.

During recent months, the South African government has moved to curb alleged Communists more severely and prevent further outbreaks of organized sabotage. It has failed, however, to make a distinction between Communists and genuine liberals and nationalists, and as a result it sharply restricts the freedoms of all South Africans.

The government has placed some thirty persons under house arrest for violation of the harsh and extremely broad "Sabotage Act," and it has published a list of more than four hundred "named Communists" who are banned from political activity under the new act. Statements made by any banned or restricted person may not be published anywhere in the country. This stricter government surveillance has not materially diminished Communist activity in South Africa, which has operated clandestinely since 1950. Moreover, the Communists have moved part of their base of operations outside the country.

One of the more unfortunate aspects of South Africa's tighter control of Communist activities is its refusal to distinguish between Communist opposition and legitimate opposition to the South African government. In their zeal to brand all opposition "Communist," they appear to be lending strength to the Communist cause. The editor of the *Rand Daily Mail,* a liberal, non-Communist newspaper, made this point very clear in a front-page editorial directed to the Minister of Justice. He wrote:

> Communism has never had wide support among non-whites in South Africa. You are giving it the stature of a mass movement . . . Do not hand to the Communists a monopoly of fighting for the rights of non-whites. For if you do these things . . . you will have sealed South Africa's fate . . . having delivered a great country into the hands of the Communists.

The attitude that opposition to the governments in power in southern Africa automatically is Communist-inspired could lead to the very type of penetration that we seek to prevent in Africa.

This brings me to one of the dilemmas the West faces today. Throughout the southern part of Africa there are a number of movements directed toward racial accommodation and self-government. These movements seek Western assistance and do not desire a commitment from the Communist world. The response of the West traditionally is to call for peaceful transition by both the disenfranchised majorities and the ruling minorities. However, if hopes for achieving legitimate demands for racial and political equality through such peaceful methods are disappointed and the question becomes one of survival for these political movements, any compunctions they might have about accepting Communist aid could be expected to disappear.

Such an eruption of African frustrations in the southern part of the continent is what the Communists are counting on in the long run. They believe that this would put the Western nations in a position where their influence and political credit among Africans will rapidly diminish.

Unless there is a discernible movement toward more progressive policies in those parts of southern Africa not enjoying majority rule—and unless there appears vigorous leadership from the West to accomplish such progress—there is a good possibility that western influence could be replaced by that of the Communists. Aided by a deterioration of the Western position, the Sino-Soviet bloc could become the leading outside influence in the painful transition in southern Africa and in the minds of Africans everywhere.

It seems to me, then, that this is a grave problem to which the entire West must give urgent priority. I am certain that the actual time we have left to work on this problem is really much shorter than we anticipate today.

At the moment, Communist tactics in Africa have not led to a direct confrontation of East and West, as in Berlin. Rather, Communist activities are mainly concerned with exploiting the opportunities offered them by white obstruction of Africa's drive for independence, with the object of putting the West in the position of seeming to oppose the black Africans for racial reasons.

The basic answer the West must give to the Communist challenge in Africa is a program of action which responds to the pressing political, economic, and social needs of the peoples of Africa, rather than simply an attack on communism. The best way to stop communism is to eliminate the conditions in which it flourishes—conditions not only of poverty, illness, illiteracy, and malnutrition, but also of lack of self-expression and self-government.

Viewed in this light, the impact of communism on African nationalism is a sharp challenge for the West. It behooves the West to meet this challenge with new determination and imagination. We bear a great responsibility to the peoples of Africa, to ourselves, and to future generations to help the peoples of southern Africa achieve and develop self-government, so that they will have a freedom and a government they will be determined to protect as their own against any kind of alien subversion. America has an historic role to play to help the African people attain and enjoy the values to which they aspire—values which, by and large, are the same as the ones we cherish.

References

INTRODUCTION

1. Bertrand de Jouvenel, "A Better Life in an Affluent Society," *Diogenes*, Vol. XXXIII (1961), p. 62.

I. GERMAN NATIONAL AND FRAGMENTATION

1. Ludwig Dehio, *Germany and World Politics* (New York: Alfred A. Knopf, 1959), pp. 11–37. See also *Gleichgewicht oder Hegemonie* (Krefeld, 1958), p. 6.

III. THE PROBLEM OF NATIONAL MINORITIES IN THE USSR

1. Hugh Seton-Watson, "Soviet National Policy," *Russian Review*, Vol. XV, pp. 3–13.
2. From the *Program of the Communist Party of the Soviet Union*, Part II, Chapter IV.
3. See Richard Pipes, "Muslims in Central Asia: Trends and Prospects," *Middle East Journal*, Vol. IX, pp. 147–62, pp. 295–308.
4. See Aleksandr Yurchenko, "The New Party Program and the Nationality Question," *Studies on the Soviet Union*, New Series, Vol. II, No. 2, pp. 17 ff.

IV. NATIONALISM IN SOUTH AFRICA

1. See *Ou en Nuwe in die Suid-Afrikaanse Geskiedskrywing* by F. A. Jaarsveld (Pretoria, 1961), pp. 48–51, for an analysis of historical works by Bantus.
2. New York: McGraw-Hill Book Co., p. 87.
3. For an examination of this policy see "Reappraisal in South Africa" by Amry Vandenbosch in the *Yale Review*, Autumn, 1963.
4. C. H. Calkin, in his interesting book, *There Are No South Africans* (London, 1941). Mr. Calkin at the time was editor of the *Natal Witness*.

REFERENCES

5. Quoted by M. S. Green in his *The Making of South Africa* (Cape Town, 1958), p. 61.

6. For an interesting and candid statement of the ideas and ideals of Afrikaner nationalism, see *Ons Volksedeaal, Drie Lesings*, by L. J. Du Plessis, T. J. Hugo, and F. J. Labuschagne (n.p., n.d.).

7. The following are a few of the publications representing this view: *Delayed Action: An Ecumenical Witness for the Afrikaans-speaking Church*, containing eleven essays by as many different writers (Pretoria, 1961); *Suid Afrika Waarheen*, by B. B. Keet (Stellenbosch, 1956); *Ras, Volk en Nasie in terme van die Skrif* (English edition titled *Principle and Practice in Race Relations According to Scripture*), by J. C. G. Kotze (Stellenbosch, 1962).

8. See Green, *op. cit.*, pp. 102 ff.

9. C. Headlam, *The Milner Papers, 1897–1905* (2 vols.; London, 1931–33), Vol. II, p. 407.

10. *Sunday Times* (Johannesburg), July 15, 1962.

11. Oswald Pirow, *J. B. M. Hertzog* (n.p., 1957), p. 259.

12. *Ibid.*

13. *House of Assembly Debates, 1961*, column 139 (January 25, 1961).

14. See D. P. Botha, *Die Opkoms Van Ons Derde Stand* (Cape Town, 1960), for a warm plea by a Dutch Reformed minister for assimilation of the coloreds with the whites.

15. See the very positive statement by Prime Minister Verwoerd in Parliament, January 24, 1961. *House of Assembly Debates, 1961*, column 89 ff.

16. Quoted in Parliament, *House of Assembly Debates, 1961*, column 156 (January 25, 1961).

17. *House of Assembly Debates, 1961*, column 179 (January 26, 1961).

18. The *Times* (Johannesburg), October 8, 1960.

19. The *Star* (Johannesburg), December 17, 1962. The motivation of the new appeal was frankly stated by a nationalist member of Parliament: "The vast majority of the whites in South Africa would like to keep the control in the hands of the white man. But we cannot retain it on our divided basis. We cannot go on in South Africa on this basis of an unnatural division between English-speaking and Afrikaans-speaking." *House of Assembly Debates, 1960*, column 3749 (March 21, 1960).

20. *Dagblad en Sondagsnuus* (Johannesburg), July 15, 1962.

110

Biographical Notes

WILLIAM J. BOSSENBROOK, Ph.D., Franklin Lecturer for 1962–63, is professor of history at Wayne State University. Born in Wisconsin in 1897, he attended Calvin College, Grand Rapids, Michigan, and was graduated from the University of Michigan in 1921. He received his Ph.D. degree from the University of Chicago in 1931. He has been associated with Wayne State University since 1931. Professor Bossenbrook is a co-author of *Foundations of Western Civilization,* Boston, 1939–40, and a contributing author to Allan Nevins and Louis M. Hacker (eds.), *The United States and Its Place in World Affairs, 1918–1943,* Boston, 1943. His most recent publication is *The German Mind,* Wayne State University Press, 1961.

HANS KOHN, Ph.D., professor of history and the leading authority on nationalism in this country, was born in Prague, Czechoslovakia, in 1891, and received his *Dr. Juris* degree from the German University of Praha in 1923. He was professor of history at Smith College, 1934–41; Sydenham Clark Parsons professor of history, 1941–49; and professor of history at City College, New York, from 1949–62, emeritus, 1962– . He has been professor and lecturer at numerous colleges, including Harvard, University of California, and the University of Colorado.

He was a Guggenheim fellow in 1940, visiting professor of international relations under the John Hay Whitney Foundation's Professors Emeriti program at the University of Denver, 1963, and a fellow at the Center for Advanced Study, Wesleyan University, Middletown, Connecticut, 1963–64. Professor Kohn is the author of many books, including *Making of the Modern French Mind*, 1955, *American Nationalism*, 1957, *Basic History of Modern Russia*, 1957, *Mind of Germany*, 1960, *The Age of Nationalism, The First Era of Global History*, 1962, and *The Idea of Nationalism*, 1944.

ALFRED G. MEYER, Ph.D., is professor of political science at Michigan State University. Born in Germany in 1920, he came to the United States in 1939 and is a naturalized citizen. He served in the U.S. Army from 1941–45. His postgraduate work was done at Harvard, where he received his M.A. degree in 1946 and his Ph.D. degree in 1950. He was a research fellow and assistant director of the Russian Research Center, Harvard, 1950–53, and director of the Research Program on History of Communist Party of Soviet Union, Columbia, 1955–57. Professor Meyer has taught history and political science at Harvard, University of Washington, Hunter College, and the Free University of Berlin. He is the author of several books dealing with Soviet history, politics, and ideology, including *Marxism: The Unity of Theory and Practice*, 1954; *Leninism*, 1957; and *Communism*, 1962.

AMRY VANDENBOSCH, Ph.D., is professor of political science, and the director of the William Andrew Patterson School of Diplomacy and International Commerce, University of Kentucky. He was born in Zeeland, Michigan, in 1894, and his postgraduate work was done at the University of Chicago, where he received his Ph.D. degree in 1926. He was head of the department of political science at the University of Kentucky from 1934 to 1958. He has been a visiting professor and lecturer at numerous universities, and was a Fulbright lecturer at Leiden, Netherlands, 1957–58. Professor Vandenbosch is interested in the role of colonialism, especially of the Dutch, in world affairs and has written a number of books on Netherlands foreign policy and the governments and politics of southeast Asia, including *Southeast Asia Among the World Powers,* 1958 (with R. A. Butwell), and *Dutch Foreign Policy Since 1815: A Study in Small Power Politics,* 1959. In 1962 he traveled extensively in Africa gathering materials on the impact of colonialism there, with particular attention to the South African situation. His most recent book, with W. N. Hogan, is *Toward World Order,* 1963.

G. MENNEN WILLIAMS, J.D., LL.D., has served in the State Department as Assistant Secretary of State for African Affairs since 1961. Born in 1911, in Detroit, Michigan, he was graduated from Princeton University in 1933. He received his J.D. degree from University of Michigan Law School in 1936. From 1942 to 1946 he served as lieutenant (j.g.), advancing to lieutenant commander, U.S.N.R., overseas. His decorations include Legion of Merit with Combat V; Presidential Unit Citation with three stars; Grand Officer of the Order of Orange Nassau (by Netherlands); Grand Commander Royal Order of Phoenix (Greece); Humane Band of African Redemption (Liberia); and Polonia Restituta (Polish government in exile). For six terms, from 1949 to 1960, he was Governor of the State of Michigan. A frequent traveler in Africa on State Department business, Mr. Williams has sought to understand sympathetically the expectations and frustrations of the new nations of Africa.

The manuscript was edited by Elvin T. Gidley. The type face for both the text and display is Baskerville originally cut in the 1750s by John Baskerville.

The book is printed on Glatfelter's RRR antique paper and bound in Fromson Orban's Elephant Hide paper over boards. Manufactured in the United States of America.